Informal Logical Fallacies

Informal Logical Fallacies

A Brief Guide

Revised Edition

Jacob E. Van Vleet

Hamilton Books

Lanham • Boulder • New York • Toronto • London

Published by Hamilton Books
An imprint of The Rowman & Littlefield Publishing Group, Inc.
4501 Forbes Boulevard, Suite 200, Lanham, Maryland 20706
Hamilton Books Acquisitions Department (301) 459-3366

6 Tinworth Street, London SE11 5AL, United Kingdom

British Library Cataloguing in Publication Information Available

Library of Congress Control Number: 2020949180

ISBN 978-0-7618-7253-5 (pbk. : alk. paper)
ISBN 978-0-7618-7254-2 (electronic)

™ The paper used in this publication meets the minimum requirements of American National Standard for Information Sciences Permanence of Paper for Printed Library Materials, ANSI/NISO Z39.48-1992.

The age of making distinctions is gone.

—S. Kierkegaard

Contents

Preface

In my fifteen years of teaching logic and critical thinking courses to undergraduates in the San Francisco Bay Area, I have found that logic textbooks created for these classes are usually quite long and inaccessible to the average reader. Furthermore, most of these textbooks spend a great deal of time covering formal logic rather than informal logic.

I designed *Informal Logical Fallacies: A Brief Guide* as an accessible supplementary text for logic or critical thinking courses. This book introduces the reader to over fifty informal logical fallacies. These fallacies are commonly found in the media today and are often used to propagate fear, blind faith, and submission. For this reason alone, it is important to become aware of informal logical fallacies. However, the ability to think critically will help one in every aspect of life.

This revised and expanded edition features new appendices, updated examples, and several additional fallacies—including a new chapter on non-Western fallacies. It is my sincere hope that this short guide will sharpen the critical thinking skills of all who read it.

Jacob E. Van Vleet
Berkeley, CA
Summer, 2020

Introduction

WHAT IS AN INFORMAL LOGICAL FALLACY?

The word fallacy comes from the Latin word *fallacia*, meaning "trick," "deceit," or "fraud." A logical fallacy is an argument containing faulty reasoning. There are two types of logical fallacies: formal and informal. A formal logical fallacy is an argument that is flawed due to an error pertaining to the *structure* of the argument. An informal logical fallacy is an argument that is flawed due to an error pertaining to the *content* of the argument. This short guide is primarily concerned with informal logical fallacies.

This book divides informal logical fallacies into five categories. First there are *linguistic fallacies*. These arguments are flawed due to a lack of clarity, as the use of vague or ambiguous terms severely weakens one's argument. Second, there are *fallacies of omission*. These arguments selectively leave out vital components or misrepresent certain positions in order to convince the listener of the correctness of the conclusion. For example, if certain options are left out of the equation, the listener may assume that only the options presented are available. Third, there are *fallacies of intrusion*. These fallacies involve an incorporation of irrelevant material in order to persuade the listener to agree with a particular claim. For example, appeals to fear or pity may convince one to accept a conclusion when these appeals have little or nothing to do with the truth of the conclusion. Fourth, there are *fallacies involving built-in assumptions*. These arguments contain assumptions about tradition, nature, and other people. Fifth, there are *causal fallacies*. These arguments rest on a misunderstanding of cause and effect. For example, one might assume that simply because events occur sequentially, they are causally related.

There are many kinds of logical fallacies within each of these five categories. Also, it is not uncommon to encounter certain fallacies that fit into more than one category. These will become clear as one reads through the explanations and examples in the following.

THE IMPORTANCE OF STUDYING INFORMAL LOGICAL FALLACIES

There are at least three main reasons for studying informal logical fallacies. First, by becoming aware of fallacies, one will be able to detect poor arguments. This is an invaluably helpful skill that will guide one through a world full of spin, propaganda, and lies.

Second, by studying informal logical fallacies, one's analytical capabilities will increase. This means that one will not only be able to recognize erroneous reasoning but will also be able to think more critically in general. The ability to think critically is crucial in nearly every aspect of life.

Finally, by studying informal logical fallacies, one can gain the confidence to challenge lazy assumptions and unquestioned beliefs. This confidence is necessary in order to think for oneself. Only by thinking for oneself will one be able to navigate life with authenticity and to genuinely approach the most important religious, political, and ethical issues of today.

WHAT IS AN ARGUMENT?

An argument is a set of statements made up of premises and a conclusion. Premises are statements containing data, facts, evidence, or any other type of support for a claim. A conclusion is a claim which rests on a premise or premises. Good arguments are made up of reliable premises and a conclusion that follows from the premises. Poor arguments usually consist of insufficient evidence, no evidence, emotional appeals, assumptions, or a host of other possible flaws. When one studies arguments, one should continually ask: "Do the premises fully support the conclusion?" As we will see in this short guide, the majority of logical fallacies contain premises which do not fully support a specific conclusion.

It should also be noted that fallacies do not always consist of premises and a conclusion. Poor arguments often neglect supporting evidence, resulting in a statement or statements which may not resemble an argument. For this reason, it is helpful to remember that fallacies take many structural forms. Furthermore, some fallacies are more accurately described as rhetorical devices rather than as arguments.

CHARACTERISTICS OF CRITICAL THINKING

This book is not simply about logical fallacies. It is also about critical thinking. Critical thinking is defined as *the careful analysis of beliefs, arguments, and positions in order to arrive at correct conclusions*. By studying logical fallacies, one will become able to distinguish poor argumentation from good argumentation. However, familiarity with logical fallacies alone is not enough to turn one into a critical thinker. There are several other important characteristics of critical thinking. Here are some:

1. Openness to the possibility of being wrong.
2. Willingness to listen to others' arguments, ideas, and beliefs.
3. Ability to listen to criticism without responding emotionally.
4. Willingness to question one's own beliefs.
5. Commitment to making an effort to truly understand others' arguments, ideas, and beliefs before opposing or criticizing them.
6. Commitment to making an effort to avoid unclear language and arguments.
7. Willingness to respect alternate views if good support is provided for these views.

All of these characteristics of critical thinking require two things: courage and hard work. First, it is sometimes threatening to question one's own beliefs and to listen to others' arguments and ideas. This does not mean critical thinking requires one to change his or her beliefs or to uncritically accept the beliefs of others. It simply means one is willing to thoughtfully analyze both.

Second, critical thinking is not easy. It takes discipline and hard work to continually question, carefully consider, and test the many claims we encounter. Many people avoid critical thinking for this very reason. It is far easier to allow someone else to think for you. However, if one wants to grow intellectually, then one will make an effort to think for oneself.

Chapter One

Linguistic Fallacies

1.1 FALLACY OF DIVISION

This is also known as the *whole-to-part fallacy*. This argument states that because the whole has a certain characteristic, the parts that make up the whole must also have the same characteristic. In other words, the fallacy of division claims the whole is always the same as its parts. The "whole" referred to might be a specific group of people, an institution, a body of literary work, or just about any other ensemble made up of individual components, pieces, or parts. For example:

Example 1:

> The Dodgers have an excellent team this year. Therefore, we can safely conclude that every player on the team is outstanding.

Example 2:

> The chocolate cake tastes sweet. All of its ingredients must be sweet.

Example 3:

> Berkeley is a very liberal city. Stan lives in Berkeley. He must be an extremely liberal person.

Example 4:

> Republicans are in favor of immigration reform. Mr. Thomas is a staunch Republican. Therefore, Mr. Thomas must be in favor of immigration reform.

It is clear the parts or ingredients of a whole do not always have the same characteristics as the whole itself. When one commits the fallacy of division, one erroneously uses the characteristics of the whole to define or categorize its constituents. Such an argument strays far from clarity, making assumptions about the parts without critically investigating them or considering them individually.

1.2 FALLACY OF COMPOSITION

This fallacy is the opposite of the fallacy of division. It is sometimes referred to as the *part-to-whole fallacy*. The fallacy of composition involves an assumption that the characteristics of the parts are identical to the characteristics of the whole. In other words, the whole is assumed to be composed of identical parts. For example:

Example 1:

> The woman who rear-ended me was Asian. All Asians must be terrible drivers.

Example 2:

> Some life forms exhibit signs of sentience. Therefore, all life forms must be sentient.

Example 3:

> The chocolate cake recipe calls for salt. It must be a salty-tasting cake.

Example 4:

> The terrorists who attacked us were Muslim. Therefore, all Muslims are terrorists.

These examples are incredibly poor arguments. If one ingredient of a recipe has a certain taste, this does not entail the final product will taste like the ingredient. Likewise, simply because a member of a group or class is a certain way, this does not necessarily mean the entire group or class is the same. Members of religions, political parties, and ethnic groups are all extremely diverse. However, due to this fallacy, stereotypical ways of thinking are common. We must be vigilantly aware of stereotypes and other fallacies of composition.

1.3 VAGUENESS

Vagueness is not an informal logical fallacy. It is however, perhaps the most common element found in unclear communication. A word or phrase is vague if it is imprecise or lacks specific clarifying details. Consider this example:

Example 1:

It is obvious that Mary Smith is special.

In this example the word "special" is not clear. Mary might be special because she is someone's lover, or because she is mentally challenged, or because she is entitled to some privilege. In any case, we cannot know because the statement is vague. Here is another example:

Example 2:

Person A: What do you do for a living?

Person B: I am an artist.

Here, we can see the word "artist" is vague. Is the person a painter? A sculptor? A songwriter? A poet? Also, in this example we see another important aspect of vagueness: people often offer vague responses in order to dodge questions. Consider these examples:

Example 3:

Judge: Where were you on the night of December fourteenth?

Defendant: I was out.

Example 4:

Veronica: How is your first semester at UC Berkeley, George?

George: Oh, you know, it is what it is.

In both cases we see vague responses that are meant to dodge the question. In example 3 the defendant states she was "out." It is unclear as to what this specifically means. In the next example George replies by stating ". . . it is what it is." This may appease Veronica; however, it is still a vague answer that does not reveal how George's first semester is going.

We must be on the lookout for ambiguous and vague words and phrases as we read the news, listen to politicians, and talk with our friends. Also, we need to try and avoid vagueness and ambiguity ourselves, despite that it is often the easiest type of communication. Speaking and writing with clarity and precision takes work, but it ultimately reveals rather than obscures the truth.

1.4 EQUIVOCATION

This fallacy occurs when one word or phrase is used in two different ways in an argument. Sometimes the fallacy of equivocation is called the *double meaning fallacy*. Equivocation always relies on an ambiguous word or phrase and draws its conclusion from this ambiguity. For example:

Example 1:

All men are created equal. Women are not men. Therefore, women are not created equal.

In this example we can see that "men" is used quite differently in the first and second sentences. In the first, "men" refers to all human beings. In the second, "men" refers to only males. This argument is clearly fallacious because it relies on two very different definitions of "men." Consider these examples:

Example 2:

Exercise is good for the heart. Johanna recently broke up with her boyfriend and says she has a broken heart. She just needs to get some exercise.

Example 3:

> Philosophers say life is ultimately a mystery. My sister loves to curl up with a good mystery. She must truly enjoy life.

Example 4:

> Everyone knows they should do what is right. I have a right to smoke. Therefore, I should smoke.

In each of these examples we can see clearly one word or phrase is used in two very different ways. We should always be aware of ambiguities and the use of double meanings. If an ambiguity or inconsistency is discovered in an argument, one should try and restate the argument in a clear manner, or one should dismiss it altogether.

1.5 WEAK ANALOGY

An analogy is a comparison of one thing with something else for the purposes of explaining or persuading. The comparison might be of two people, events, places, or just about anything else. For example, one might say, "Seattle is like a cleaner version of San Francisco." Here the comparison between two cities is clear and straightforward. However, some analogies are unclear, unhelpful, or downright nonsensical. These are called weak analogies. For example:

Example 1:

> Renting a house, rather than buying, is like flushing your money down the toilet.

In reality, renting is not simply throwing away money as the argument suggests—even if it does not end in investment or ownership. Rather, renting is paying for the temporary use of property or a good. Many people use rented cars, houseboats, and textbooks, among other things. Using something you've paid for is not the same as "flushing your money down the toilet." Here are two more examples of weak analogies:

Example 2:

> Denying the existence of God is like refusing to believe the sky is blue.

Example 3:

Recycling is like putting a band-aid on a broken arm.

In these examples, the analogies given are unclear and unhelpful. Furthermore, the two things compared in each argument have nothing in common. We must strive to avoid using faulty analogies, and we must always be on the lookout for weak comparisons.

1.6 PSEUDO-PROFUNDITY

This fallacy is found when a statement appears to be insightful and profound, but in reality, it is unclear and incoherent. We hear supposedly wise and weighty proclamations quite regularly from New Age gurus, televangelists, and college professors. But many of these statements, on closer inspection, are so vague they might as well be meaningless. For example:

Example 1:

Guru: Reality does not exist; we exist on the shore of a collective nightmare.

Example 2:

Professor: My philosophy is that the ALL becomes the ONE which is identical to the Self and to the Cosmos through which knowledge is attained.

At first glance these statements appear intellectually deep. However, they lack clarity and specificity. Furthermore, each can be interpreted in a variety of ways. This can lead to multiple contradictory views, which in turn cause confusion.

The philosopher Martin Heidegger was often accused of committing the fallacy of pseudo-profundity. For example, Paul Edwards believes Heidegger's philosophy is a perfect example of pseudo-profundity; or as Edwards puts it, "hideous gibberish."[1] Consider these excerpts from Heidegger's work:

Example 3:

Is Being a mere word and its meaning a vapor, or does what is designated by the word 'Being' hold within it the historical destiny of the West?[2]

Example 4:

> We are ourselves the entities to be analyzed. The Being of any such entity is in each case mine. These entities, in their Being, comport themselves towards their Being. As entities with such Being, they are delivered over to their own Being. Being is that which is an issue for every such entity.[3]

It should be noted that scholars continue to debate Heidegger's work. These statements from Heidegger may be insightful or profoundly meaningful, but there is no way of knowing without further information from his writings. In any case, we must make it our goal to speak with clarity and coherence rather than vagueness and imprecision. Furthermore, we must listen critically to the statements of others, looking for clearness before assuming their words are profound or true—even when the speaker is an authority figure.

1.7 INFLATION

The fallacy of inflation occurs when one inflates the importance of the issue they are discussing, either for personal reasons, or for rhetorical manipulation. Not to be confused with hyperbole, it is often encountered when one states dogmatically that the topic under discussion is without qualification more significant than any other topic being discussed. For example:

Example 1:

> The reason we should be talking about global warming is because it is the greatest threat to humankind in history.

Example 2:

> The Holy Scripture should be studied and taught. Why? Because the Bible is the most significant book ever written.

Example 3:

> We must fight for stricter drinking laws. Alcoholism is the most urgent social dilemma facing us today.

There is no doubt global warming is a serious threat. There is also no question that religious scriptures have vital cultural significance or that alcoholism is a social ill. However, in each of these examples the importance of each topic is greatly inflated to serve the purposes of the person making the claim.

1.8 FALSE CERTAINTY

More of a rhetorical device than a logical fallacy, this occurs when one insinuates something is guaranteed, when it is not. This is often referred to as false certainty. Quite commonly found in sales or politics, it can be seen in the following examples:

Example 1:

> Without a shadow of a doubt, we are certain this new policy will make us safer than we were in previous years—to a greater or lesser degree.

Example 2:

> To me, the resolution is a safe bet: one I definitely feel is the right move to make. Therefore, you should agree with me.

Example 3:

> It has been demonstrated conclusively that this soda is 100% delicious and safe for nearly all consumers.

In each of these examples, words and phrases such as "certain" and "demonstrated conclusively," are followed or preceded by qualifiers such as "to me," and "nearly." This rhetorical technique can be quite effective. The emphasis on the language of certainty often takes precedence in the listener's mind, overshadowing the terms that negate the certainty. It should also be noted that these examples are not technically lies. The person presenting the claim makes sure to qualify his or her statement, leaving a back door out in case their "guarantee" does not come to pass.

1.9 FALLACY OF DEFINITION

There are many different types of the fallacy of definition. Here, the type we will discuss occurs when one purports to "define" a term; however, instead of correctly defining the term, they describe it in a way which serves their purposes. Or, on occasion the term will be "defined" in a way intended to manipulate the listener or audience. For example:

Example 1:

Democracy is defined as getting off your ass and getting involved!

Example 2:

Let me explain the discipline of philosophy: It is defined as the spouting of nonsense.

Example 3:

Privilege is defined as thinking something is not a problem because it is not a problem to you!

In each of these examples, we see two common characteristics. First, the definition of the term is incorrect. Second, the definition given is biased or manipulative. It is important to remember that definitions should be as clear and thorough as possible, without vagueness, ambiguity, or hinting at coercion. If a definition fails to meet these criteria, one should be cautious.

NOTES

1. Paul Edwards, "Heidegger's Quest for Being." In the Journal *Philosophy*, 1989. p. 468.
2. Martin Heidegger, *An Introduction to Metaphysics*. Translated by Ralph Mannheim. New Haven: Yale University Press, 1972. p. 42.
3. Martin Heidegger, *Being and Time*. Translated by John Macquarrie and Edward Robinson. New York: Harper Collins, 1962. p. 42.

Chapter Two

Fallacies of Omission

2.1 BIFURCATION

The fallacy of bifurcation is also known as the *black-and-white fallacy*. This fallacy occurs when the arguer presents the listener with only two choices (hence the prefix *bi*), when in fact there are other possibilities to choose from. In other words, the argument limits the options of choices, omitting possible alternatives. The fallacy of bifurcation usually takes the following form:

Premise: There are only two options: x and y.

Conclusion: Option x is false; therefore, option y must be true.

We can see clearly that, if there were indeed only two options, the argument would be valid. The fallacy occurs when the argument concerns factual human categories rather than merely logical symbols. For example:

Example 1:

You are either a Republican or a Democrat. You are not a Republican, so you must be a Democrat.

In this example only two political parties are presented in the premise, when in reality there are many others that should be considered: Green, Socialist, Libertarian, Independent, etc. The fallacy of bifurcation can also be found in *loaded questions* or assertions, which in themselves are not arguments. For example:

Example 2:

You are either with us or against us.

Example 3:

There are only two types of people in this country: those who love America and those who hate it.

Example 4:

Are you religious or are you an atheist?

Example 5:

Since you are critical of capitalism, you must be a socialist.

In all of these examples the options are limited. This fallacy is commonly used by politicians in order to manipulate people. We often hear of "liberal versus conservative," "us versus them," "good versus evil," and "pro-war versus anti-war," when in fact there are other positions that need to be seriously considered. The fallacy of bifurcation is always an oversimplification of a more complex issue.

2.2 FALSE DILEMMA

Like the fallacy of bifurcation, the false dilemma erroneously limits options. In fact, the bifurcation is a type of false dilemma. However, whereas the bifurcation limits the choices to only two, this fallacy may limit the options to three or more when, in reality, there are other alternatives that should be considered. For example:

Example 1:

A restaurant menu reads: "We have meals for all diets: vegetarian, vegan, and meat eaters."

In this example, the options are limited to three, when in fact there are more types of diets than these. Some people follow religious dietary guidelines; some cannot eat gluten products; some only eat organic foods. Here is a very different example of the false dilemma:

Example 2:

Jesus was either a liar, a lunatic, or Lord.

This example is a common argument for the divinity of Christ. However, this statement limits the choices when there are other possibilities that should be considered. One alternate possibility, according to Muslims, is that Jesus was a prophet. Another alternative—albeit unlikely—is that Jesus never existed. In any case, all possibilities should be considered in an honest and open manner. Here are some final examples of the false dilemma:

Example 3:

College students are either working toward an associate's degree, a bachelor's degree, or a master's degree.

Example 4:

Professor to students: Do you believe in creationism, evolutionary theory, or intelligent design?

Example 5:

Are you a size small, medium, or large?

We should be aware of the false dilemma fallacy. One way to do this is by remembering that people, places, and events are often more complex than they seem.

2.3 ARGUMENTUM AD IGNORANTIAM

Argumentum ad ignorantiam is Latin for "argument from ignorance." This is an argument that uses a lack of proof or evidence to convince the listener the subject in question cannot be taken seriously or should be discounted completely. Often the lack of proof or evidence is meant to imply a refutation. The structure of this argument takes the following form:

Premise: There is no evidence or proof for x.

Conclusion: x is false; x should be dismissed; or x has been refuted.

The argumentum ad ignorantiam fallacy is quite common in religious discussions. Consider this well-known example:

Example 1:

> The existence of God has never been disproved. Therefore, God must exist.

One of the serious problems with the ad ignorantiam fallacy is that in many cases its opposite can be argued in the same manner. For example:

Example 2:

> The existence of God has never been proven. Therefore, God does not exist.

Simply because there is not verifiable evidence that a certain thing exists, this does not mean its existence should be dismissed or not taken seriously. More importantly, we must remember that *a lack of proof is not a refutation.* Here are three final examples:

Example 3:

> Candidate Smith has never spoken out concerning her views on abortion. We can safely conclude she must be pro-choice.

Example 4:

> There is no proof extraterrestrials exist. Therefore, they must be figments of our imagination.

Example 5:

> Since we have no physical evidence supporting the claim that Socrates was a real person, he must have never existed.

Here we see a lack of evidence is used to dismiss the issue at hand. In some cases, this lack of proof is used to argue for the opposing position. When we encounter little or no evidence in support of an assertion or claim, we should be honest with ourselves instead of jumping to hasty conclusions. It is far better to admit we do not have all the information needed to make an informed judgment, than to make arguments from ignorance.

2.4 SHIFTING THE BURDEN OF PROOF

Shifting the burden of proof is usually used as a response to a particular argument. It is a type of argumentum ad ignorantiam. This is an argument maintaining that because one cannot defend one's position, it must be incorrect or false. For example:

Example 1:

Lawyer: My client did not rob the bank last Friday. Prove that he did!

In this example, the lawyer rests his argument on the sole basis that his client cannot be proven guilty. However, as is the case with the argumentum ad ignorantiam, the lack of evidence in no way acts as a refutation of the argument's claim. Consider these examples:

Example 2:

Brian: The CIA is in charge of cocaine distribution in the United States.

Alex: That sounds unlikely. What evidence do you have supporting this theory?

Brian: Prove that it isn't so!

Example 3:

Preacher: God wants everyone to donate money to my ministry.

Congregant: I do not think that is what God wants.

Preacher: Well, provide evidence God doesn't want it.

The burden of proof in each of these examples is shifted from the arguer onto the opponent. However, it is not the job of the opponent to disprove the arguer's position. It is always the arguer's task to provide solid evidence in support of his or her case. Without evidence, the arguer is simply making unsupported assertions.

2.5 STRAW ARGUMENT

The straw argument was originally named the *straw man argument*. It is an argument that intentionally presents a misrepresentation of a particular position in order to easily refute or dismiss it. A straw man is easier to knock down than a real person, hence the name. For example:

Example 1:

> Jews and Christians simply believe that if you are good you will go to heaven, and if you are evil you will go to hell. This is the gist of their belief. So, you shouldn't take them seriously.

Here the views of Jews and Christians are intentionally distorted so they can be easily dismissed. However, one with an eye for fallacious argumentation will recognize the argument rests on an oversimplification. The theological beliefs of Jews and Christians are far more complicated than what is stated in the argument. Consider these final examples:

Example 2:

> Anarchism is a political ideology stating that everyone should run around and fornicate in the streets. It is for this reason I reject anarchism.

Example 3:

> The democratic position today is essentially a fascist and communist stance. So, if you are in favor of Communism and fascism, you will vote for the Democratic Party.

In both of these straw arguments, a misrepresentation is used in order to easily discredit or reject a position. We must be careful when we encounter one who claims to refute a position he or she finds disagreeable. Often this is not a refutation of the actual position, but a refutation of a perversion of the position.

2.6 REDUCTIONISM

Reductionism occurs when one reduces a complex phenomenon to a single fact that may or may not be related to that phenomenon. This is often done in order to explain a many-sided or multifaceted issue, event, or belief system. Reductionism is regularly found in explanatory statements given for involved occurrences or systems of thought such as religion, politics, or science. Consider these examples:

Example 1:

Religion is simply a response to economic inequality.

Example 2:

Science is essentially determinism.

Example 3:

Politics is nothing more than a power struggle.

Here we see the basic structure of the fallacy of reductionism: x (a complex issue) is nothing more than y (a simple, often vague, explanation). This is similar to the straw argument. The difference is this: the straw argument intentionally misrepresents a particular point of view in order to dismiss it, whereas reductionism often involves an over generalized explanation that precludes other explanatory factors. This may or may not be intentional, but like the straw argument, it is certainly intellectually lazy.

Reductionism is a clear example of a fallacy of omission. All fallacies of omission leave out important information rather than attempting to explore and discuss the various aspects of the issue at hand.

2.7 FALLACY OF PSYCHOLOGISM

This fallacy is a type of reductionism. It might also be categorized as a causal fallacy. The fallacy of psychologism occurs when one reduces another's actions, beliefs, or desires to nothing more than a psychological mechanism or an unconscious fear or desire. For example:

Example 1:

You are only a conservative because you unconsciously want someone to have strict control over your behavior.

Example 2:

Maria isn't consciously aware of it, but her belief in karma stems from her hidden desire for order and structure.

Example 3:

> Samuel only believes his religion because he has an irrational fear of displeasing his mother.

The explanations in these examples may be partially correct. However, in reality, there is no discernable, verifiable evidence that deeply laden psychological influences have determined the beliefs of the individuals in the examples. Furthermore, while it may be true that psychological influences are present in humans, it does not follow that all significant motivations and concerns stem from unconscious desires and fears.

It should also be noted that the fallacy of psychologism is not the same as psychologism in epistemology and metaphysics. Both of the latter concern the foundations of logical laws and mathematics. The former is defined and explained above.

2.8 PERFECTIONIST FALLACY

This fallacy is committed when a person argues that a task or a goal should not be attempted because the possibility of reaching the goal or accomplishing the task is unlikely. This argument is heard quite often when one rejects a certain business or political proposal due to the improbability of attaining it with perfection. For example:

Example 1:

> We will never be able to fully eradicate crime on the streets of Oakland; consequently, we should not waste our time and energy trying.

Example 2:

> To create a coffee company that can truly compete with Java House is impossible. Therefore, we should not open a coffee shop.

In other words, the perfectionist fallacy states: if you cannot do something perfectly (or if you cannot finish something), then you should not even attempt it. This assumes there is a *right way* to reach a goal, and the end result is more important than the process or experience of working toward it. Another way of stating this fallacy is as follows: if you can't do x in a particular manner, then you shouldn't do it at all. Here are some final examples:

Example 3:

My artwork will never be as good as Picasso's or Chagall's. Hence, I will not waste my time with it.

Example 4:

I keep going back to cigarettes. I have tried to quit so many times, but I can't. I'll always struggle with this. So, I guess I'll keep smoking.

Example 5:

If you cannot be a perfect husband, then why do you want to get married in the first place?

Example 6:

I'll never be fluent in French, so I dropped my French class.

One of the main problems with this fallacy is its assumption that there is a universal definition of perfection, and that our actions should meet this definition and should be one hundred percent complete. In reality, many human goals or tasks get their value from the process of learning or making an effort rather than from their end results.

2.9 FALLACY OF THE UNKNOWABLE FACT

The fallacy of the unknowable fact contains as one of its premises a claim that is unknowable. This fallacy uses as evidence a "fact"—often speculation—that cannot be verified at the present time. For example:

Example 1:

Father to daughter: If you do not go to college, then you'll never be successful.

In this example, the father is claiming he knows what the future holds for his daughter. However, the future is unknown, therefore there is no way to verify or falsify the father's claim. Consider this example:

Example 2:

If only Adolf Hitler had a healthy relationship with his parents, World War II would have never occurred.

No matter what one finds out about Hitler's relationship with his parents, one cannot know how this relationship influenced his political decisions, let alone world history. To include this type of claim in one's argument is to include unverifiable data. In order to argue well, one must avoid appealing to the unknowable. Here are two final examples of the fallacy of the unknowable fact:

Example 3:

> I wish I'd gone to dental school instead of majoring in art. I'd be rich now!

Example 4:

> Elizabeth should have married Stan instead of Wayne. She would be so much happier.

2.10 WILLED IGNORANCE

More of a diversionary tactic than a logical fallacy, willed ignorance remains a common response to rational argumentation. Willed ignorance occurs when one simply refuses to engage in logical discourse or critical thinking, maintaining his or her beliefs about the issue are the final and absolute answer. This often occurs in scientific, political, or religious discussions. For example:

Example 1:

> Person A: It seems to me there are contradictions in the New Testament regarding the status and role of women.
>
> Person B: Well, what the Bible says is true—end of conversation!

Example 2:

> Person A: There seem to be some inconsistencies in Einstein's theory of relativity.
>
> Person B: Einstein was a genius, and what he said is indisputable, period.

Example 3:

> Person A: After reading the *Republic*, I believe Plato is endorsing totalitarianism.

Person B: You have no idea what you are talking about, and I will not discuss Plato's work with you.

Willed ignorance is simply an inflexible, uncritical, unquestioning attitude that refuses to listen to the other side of an argument. A fundamental prerequisite for critical thinking is the ability to carefully and patiently consider various alternatives to the issue at hand. Critical thinking requires reflection and analysis of various viewpoints. This does not mean all positions are correct—not at all! This simply means one should avoid willed ignorance, and instead carefully analyze all arguments.

Chapter Three

Fallacies of Intrusion

3.1 ARGUMENTUM AD HOMINEM, ABUSIVE

Argumentum ad hominem is translated as "argument against the person." The abusive form of this fallacy occurs when name-calling, slander or insults directed at a particular person are interjected into an argument. These are often used in order to manipulate the listener or audience. Usually, evidence or solid premises are substituted with personal attacks. Yet, on occasion, good premises are augmented with name-calling or derogatory terms. This is purely a psychological technique. It has nothing to do with solid reasoning or logical argumentation. Here are some examples of the abusive ad hominem fallacy:

Example 1:

> Candidate Greenstein is a bleeding-heart, unpatriotic liberal. Therefore, we cannot trust him as our leader.

Example 2:

> Professor Dreyfus is an arrogant jerk! You should not take his English class.

Example 3:

> Why should I listen to your political arguments? You are nothing but a big loser.

Example 4:

How can we trust a cultural Marxist to teach our children about American history?

Here we see premises (and a loaded question) incorporating name-calling instead of valid reasons. One encounters this fallacy quite regularly in political campaigns, radio talk shows, and conversations with family and friends. Even though the abusive ad hominem fallacy can be entertaining and even effective, it still relies on personal attacks rather than solid premises. For this reason alone, this argument should be avoided.

3.2 ARGUMENTUM AD HOMINEM, CIRCUMSTANTIAL

The ad hominem circumstantial fallacy, like the abusive version, seeks to attack the arguer rather than the argument. However, instead of resorting to personal attacks, an attempt is made to discredit the arguer's position by implying he or she has impure or selfish motives. For example:

Example 1:

You should not listen to Professor Miller's arguments for faculty salary increases. The only reason he is arguing for a pay raise is because he will benefit from it.

In this example we see that, rather than his actual arguments being examined or critiqued, Professor Miller himself is being attacked. It claims Miller has selfish motives for arguing in a certain manner, and because of this his arguments should be dismissed. The circumstantial fallacy does not only attack arguers and dismiss their specific arguments, as in the example above, but it can also be used to discredit any position or stance one might hold. For example:

Example 2:

Julie only accepted Harold's invitation to dinner because she felt sorry for him. There's no way she actually likes him.

Example 3:

It is obvious Aunt Sue's Christmas gift to Emma was given with ulterior motives. She gave her an airline gift certificate, but she might as well have just asked Emma to come babysit.

Example 4:

I will not accept the administration's arguments for war. Clearly, the only reason the President wants to be in the Middle East is to secure natural resources.

In all of these examples, the arguments or actions alone are not taken seriously because certain circumstances have supposedly corrupted the source of each argument or action. We need to remember that not all arguments are presented with ulterior motives and that arguments should, if possible, be analyzed by themselves, apart from their sources.

3.3 ARGUMENTUM AD HOMINEM, POSTMORTEM

This fallacy is committed when one argues that if a certain philosopher, scientist, or any other great thinker of the past were alive today, he or she would engage in an ad hominem attack. This fallacy is heard quite often on college campuses—coming from students and professors alike. For example:

Example 1:

Person A: (Offers an interpretation or idea about an issue.)

Person B: (Responding) If Nietzsche were here, he would call you an idiot!

Example 2:

Person A: (States a critique of Plato's philosophy.)

Person B: (Responding) If Plato were here, he would say your mind is not fit for learning and you should simply be a laborer.

Example 3:

Person A: (Questions and objects to a Freudian theory.)

Person B: (Responding) Well, Freud would say you are a sexually repressed jackass!

The postmortem ad hominem attack always uses an authority figure of the past (quite often someone who is dead, hence *post mortem*) to attack a person, idea, or argument. This fallacy is very easy to recognize. It almost always begins with, "If [person x] were here, he/she would say . . ." This is fallacious because of the impossibility of being able to know what someone would say here and now, in our current historical and social context. We have no way of knowing what Plato, Nietzsche, or any other great thinker of the past might say if they were engaged in a philosophical discussion with someone at the present time. Even if we feel we are an authority on an influential thinker, this does not mean we necessarily know what his/her exact response to an idea, issue, or argument would be today.

3.4 ARGUMENTUM AD VERECUNDIAM

Argumentum ad verecundiam is often translated from the Latin as "argument from authority." This fallacy relies on a false authority figure as support for a particular claim. A false authority is one who has little or no expertise in the particular context in which he or she is being used. The ad verecundiam argument can be found quite regularly in advertising. Often, celebrities, entertainers, or athletes will promote certain items or products of which they have no in-depth knowledge. For example, one might encounter a movie star selling pharmaceuticals, or a country singer promoting a politician.

A legitimate authority is one who is an expert in the appropriate field. For example, when a doctor states a certain medication is needed, the patient should seriously consider this advice. Or, if a professor of mathematics states an algebraic equation ought to be done in a certain way, the student should listen. If, however, one's doctor is preaching about religion, or if one's mathematics professor is pontificating about politics, both would be considered illegitimate, or at least questionable, authorities. There are many other examples of the ad verecundiam fallacy. Consider the following:

Example 1:

According to my grandmother, UC Berkeley is not a respected university. So, you should reconsider attending in the fall.

Example 2:

I know democracy is the most moral form of government. Only last week, my pastor presented a sermon on the moral superiority of democracy.

Example 3:

My literature professor gave a wonderful lecture on atheism. He is an expert, so he must be right.

Example 4:

For the last month, I have had headaches, nausea, and chills. I considered going to the doctor, but my mother says I just need to rest. So, I have decided to rest more. Mom knows best.

In these examples false authorities are appealed to. When creating good arguments authorities may be used, however, they should be experts in the related field. Also, with this in mind, one must always remember that even experts can be wrong.

3.5 ARGUMENTUM AD BACULUM

In ancient Rome, a rod called a baculum was carried by each leader to symbolize his power. Named after this practice, the argumentum ad baculum fallacy is also known as the *argument from the rod*, or often it is simply referred to as the *argument from fear*. The ad baculum argument uses threats, punishment or scare tactics to convince the listener to accept the conclusion of the argument. In short, fear replaces or is added to the premises or conclusion in order to psychologically manipulate the intended audience. The ad baculum fallacy usually takes the following form:

Premise: Arguer presents his or her position, which includes threats or scare tactics.

Conclusion: The arguer's position must be taken seriously, or else harm may ensue.

Yet the ad baculum argument can also be found in many other forms. The common factor is always the appeal to fear. For example:

Example 1:

Sue, if you don't go out with me, remember that I know where your family lives.

Example 2:

If we don't take care of the terrorists, then our children and grandchildren will live in constant threat of being attacked.

Example 3:

No matter where you live, you are never safe from West Nile Virus. Therefore, you should buy the new West Nile Virus protective lotion available at your local drug store.

The appeal to fear can be a very powerful and effective form of argumentation. Politicians, preachers, and parents often use ad baculum arguments. We must remember, however, that threats and scare tactics do not constitute solid premises.

3.6 APPEAL TO COMMON KNOWLEDGE

This fallacy occurs when solid premises are replaced with the fact that a belief is well known. It is sometimes referred to as the *every child knows fallacy* because it can include statements like, "even a child knows this," or, "this is so obvious, even a child would recognize it." Often the arguer will even appeal to "everyone" in his or her premises. However, the fact that something is widely accepted as true does not establish the truth of a conclusion. Here are some variations of this fallacy:

Example 1:

The earth is millions of years old. How do I know this? Because everyone knows this!

Example 2:

Even a small child can recognize morality and immorality. So, you cannot act as if all human behavior is morally ambiguous.

Example 3:

Come on, everyone knows Governor Wilkins is the best candidate for the position.

Example 4:

Of course you should accept the promotion. I can hardly believe you're asking for advice. We all know money improves the quality of life.

As demonstrated in these examples, the arguer committing this fallacy uses an appeal to common knowledge rather than providing solid evidence for a claim. While this fallacy is heard everyday—it is indeed the backbone of peer pressure and the latest cultural trends—we must remember its inherent faulty reasoning.

3.7 GENETIC FALLACY

The genetic fallacy is an argument assuming a statement, position, or idea must be flawed if the source of the statement, position, or idea is flawed (or believed to be flawed). Often the genetic fallacy is an attempt to dismiss or refute another's position based solely on the origin of the position. The genetic fallacy usually has the following form:

Premise: x originated from y.

Conclusion: x must have similarities to y and therefore cannot be taken seriously.

This argument assumes x is like y (presumably negative) simply because it came from y. This is flawed reasoning. Consider these examples of the genetic fallacy:

Example 1:

Why should we liberals not listen to Mr. Daniels? Because Mr. Daniels is from a very conservative town in the Midwest.

Example 2:

I will not vote for Schroeder. Everyone knows she is German, and we all know German history. No antisemitic candidates for me!

In these examples, people are dismissed based on the erroneous assumption they necessarily share certain negative (or perceived as negative) characteristics with their places of origin. We must remember that a person or position should never be dismissed solely on the basis of origination. A position or argument should be judged on the basis of its strength or validity, not on its source.

3.8 ARGUMENTUM AD POPULUM

Argumentum ad populum, or *argument from the people*, is a fallacy that appeals to a group of people's beliefs, tastes, or values. The people appealed to can be a small group, such as an individual clique or church group, or it can be a large group of people such as Republicans, Baptists, or feminists. The argumentum ad populum fallacy states that because a group holds a particular belief, attitude or value, this must lend support to the correctness of that belief, attitude or value. Also, the ad populum argument often claims that because the group is a certain way, the listener should accept the group's manner or action—or at least consider it as valid. For example:

Example 1:

> The Southern Baptist Convention maintains the Bible is inerrant. Therefore, you should also defend the inerrancy of the Bible.

Example 2:

> The Democratic Party endorses candidate Fuller for president. Because you are a registered Democrat, you should support candidate Fuller.

Example 3:

> Our family has always acted in manner x. Since you are part of this family you should act in manner x as well.

In these examples, a group is appealed to as the authority on a particular issue. The fallacy occurs in assuming the group is correct. Often the opinions of groups can be wrong. Consider outdated scientific and mythological beliefs. Consider forms of racism, sexism, and fascism practiced by many groups. Simply because a group of people hold a certain set of beliefs to be correct, this does not in any way imply the accurateness of these beliefs.

Argumentum ad populum is also known as the *democratic fallacy*. In a democracy, laws are passed, and officials are given offices by the consensus of the largest number of people. However, simply because a large group of voters believe one course of action to be the best, this does not ensure that the vote of the majority is necessarily correct or right. Beliefs, attitudes, and values need to be closely examined separately from the groups that support them. No matter who or how many people hold a certain belief, their advocacy does not prove its correctness.

3.9 APPEAL TO TRADITION

This fallacy is an argument that appeals to tradition or custom as justification for its conclusion. Traditions and customs can be admirable and are sometimes helpful when making decisions and formulating arguments. However, these alone do not provide solid premises for an argument. For example:

Example 1:

You should vote for a Republican. Your father and his father were both dedicated Republicans, so you should be too.

Example 2:

Mother to daughter: Our family has been Roman Catholic for many generations. How can you even consider leaving the church?

Example 3:

It has always been our custom to treat women this way. How can you challenge our customs?

Example 4:

Religious seeker: How can you be certain your religious text is accurate?

Guru: Because our tradition tells us it is.

In each of these examples an appeal to tradition is found. The error in appealing solely to tradition is this: tradition by itself is not infallible. There have been many defective traditions (not to mention unjust and harmful ones). Simply because an idea or way of life has been a tradition, this does not guarantee it is correct.

3.10 TU QUOQUE

Tu quoque is translated from the Latin as "you too." This fallacy is often used as a response to a particular claim, argument or suggestion. The tu quoque fallacy occurs when one charges another with hypocrisy or inconsistency in order to avoid taking the other's position seriously. For example:

Example 1:

Mother: You should stop smoking. It's harmful to your health.

Daughter: Why should I listen to you? You started smoking when you were sixteen.

In this example, the daughter commits the tu quoque fallacy. She dismisses her mother's argument because she believes her mother is speaking in a hypocritical manner. While the mother may indeed be inconsistent, this does not invalidate her argument. Liars, manipulators, and even hypocritical parents can create good arguments. As with the genetic fallacy, one should not dismiss an argument based on its source. Consider these examples:

Example 2:

Father: You should not drink until you are twenty-one. It's unsafe and it's illegal.

Son: How can I take you seriously? I know for a fact you drank when you were underage.

Example 3:

Teacher: One should always recycle paper, plastic and glass products. It's good for the earth and it's good for future generations.

Student: Ha! I saw you throw your soda bottle in the trash after lunch! Why should we listen to someone who doesn't practice what she preaches?

As critical thinkers, we must consider the argument itself, separate from its source. This is often hard to do. In any case, the argument must be left to stand or fall on its own, regardless of hypocrisy or inconsistency on the part of the arguer.

3.11 TWO WRONGS MAKE A RIGHT

This fallacy often assumes that because an unethical act has been committed, committing the same act again will somehow correct the initial unethical behavior. Simply repeating wrong behavior does not make it right. Like the tu quoque fallacy, the two wrongs make a right fallacy is often used to rationalize undesirable conduct. For example:

Example 1:

Sharon: Why do you keep lying to your husband?

Amanda: Because he has been lying to me for years.

Example 2:

Jim: How can you live with yourself, knowing you have killed five people in cold blood?

Gene: The state kills people every day; it's called the death penalty!

Example 3:

Forrest: Aren't you going to return the wallet you found?

Elliot: Why should I? When I lost my wallet, no one returned mine.

In these examples an assumption is made that unethical behavior is somehow justified because others previously engaged in the same or similar conduct. We must remember this type of argumentation is seriously flawed. Mimicking other's actions does not justify one's own behavior.

3.12 RED HERRING

This fallacy gets its name from a practice once used in hunting. In order to hone their dogs' tracking skills, hunters would drag a herring across the hunting path, creating a distracting smell that might lead the dogs away from the correct path. The hunters would then train the dogs to avoid the distracting smell and to follow only the scent they were instructed to follow. Like this practice, the red herring fallacy incorporates a distraction—an irrelevant issue—in order to divert attention away from the topic under discussion. For example:

Example 1:

> Lawyer: Your honor, I know my client murdered the bank teller. However, my client should not receive the maximum penalty. She was abandoned as a child, abused in foster homes, homeless by the age of ten, and she is currently addicted to drugs and alcohol. She is already suffering a great deal. She deserves mercy.

In this example, the lawyer incorporates irrelevant issues in order to divert the judge's attention away from the crime. These issues may be persuasive; however, they are irrelevant to the topic at hand: murder. The hardships of the defendant's life do not change the fact that she murdered someone. (In addition to a red herring, this example is an ad misericordiam fallacy.) Consider these examples:

Example 2:

> Police officer: Why do you have cocaine in your back pocket?
>
> Man: I was released from prison last night. I can't go back!
>
> Police officer: Please answer my question. Why do you have cocaine in your back pocket?
>
> Man: I really like your wristwatch. Where did you get it?

Example 3:

> Wife: I cannot believe you forgot Valentine's Day again.
>
> Husband: Did I tell you how beautiful you look in that dress?

Example 4:

> Student: Professor, you believe our political system is profoundly flawed. Can you please explain your reasoning?
>
> Professor: Your question reminds me of a trip I once took to Ecuador . . . (The professor goes on to tell a story without answering the question.)

In these examples an irrelevant issue is incorporated into the discussion in order to divert attention away from the topic at hand. This is precisely the goal of the red herring fallacy.

A popular form of the red herring fallacy is sometimes known as "*whataboutism*." On occasion it also takes the form of a tu quoque fallacy. This is often employed as a response to a claim or argument, bringing up a separate issue as a distraction. For example:

Example 1:

> Kristopher: I have been studying modern China and am quite appalled at China's long history of human rights violations. You should look at the data. I think you will agree with me.
>
> Johanna: What about human rights violations here in the United States? We have an atrocious history of human rights violations. We have more people imprisoned than China!

Example 2:

> Journalist: How can you justify your economic policy? It has directly resulted in unemployment and suffering for thousands of people.
>
> Politician: What about my predecessor? His policies caused more unemployment than mine!

Example 3:

> Judge: You have been accused of lying under oath and tampering with evidence. What do you have to say for yourself?
>
> Defendant: What about Mr. Smith? When he was in my position, he did far worse things! Why don't we talk about Mr. Smith?

As we can see, each of these whataboutisms are versions of the red herring fallacy. In each case, the respondent replies, "What about . . . ," bringing up another topic, without responding to the initial claim or accusation. These responses are much easier than actually dealing with the details of the preceding claims. It is also a sly way of changing the subject. In any form, the red herring is a fallacious rhetorical technique that certainly needs to be recognized and called out.

3.13 IGNORATIO ELENCHI

Ignoratio elenchi is often used as a blanket term for numerous fallacies, and is commonly known as "*missing the point.*" Ignoratio elenchi means "ignorance of the refutation" or "ignorance of the proof." Aristotle's *Sophistical Refutations*—the first book in the Western intellectual tradition discussing logical fallacies—offers the clearest explanation of ignoratio elenchi: it is an argument which draws the wrong (and often irrelevant) conclusion from the premise/s. For example:

Example 1:

> The number of car accidents is increasing exponentially. Therefore, more people must be encouraged to work from home.

Example 2:

> There is a growing rate of college students dropping out before completing a degree. That is why we need to get rid of all prerequisite math and English classes.

In each of these examples, the conclusions are irrelevant to the issue at hand. If car accidents and college completion rates are problems, then these issues must be addressed directly and investigated thoroughly, without jumping to conclusions that miss the point of the issue at hand.

In a slightly different version, the ignoratio elenchi fallacy is encountered as a response to a claim or argument. For example:

Example 3:

> Judge: Where were you and your wife on the night of March 28th?
>
> Defendant: I will not answer your question. My relationship with my wife is none of your business.

Example 4:

> Student: Why did you give me a zero on my philosophy essay?
>
> Professor: Because you submitted it three weeks late.
>
> Student: But I worked really hard on the essay and incorporated strong arguments, just like you requested.

In these examples we find clear illustrations of missing the point. In the first, the judge is inquiring about the whereabouts of the defendant, not his relationship with his wife. In the second example, the point is that the essay was turned in late, not that a great deal of work went into writing the essay. It should also be noted that the ignoratio elenchi often takes the form of a red herring, as the examples above indicate.

3.14 ARGUMENTUM AD CRUMENAM

Crumena is Latin for a purse that stores money. The argumentum ad crumenam assumes wealth, money, or possessions are the measure of the correctness of an argument. For example:

Example 1:

> We should carefully consider Senator Montgomery's political position. He was a very successful entrepreneur before he became a senator.

Example 2:

> Emily must be doing something right. Just look at all the nice clothes she has.

Example 3:

> Bill Gates dropped out of college and then became one of the wealthiest people alive. He must have known what he was talking about.

In these examples it is assumed a person's position is somehow more correct due to the wealth or possessions he or she has. However, simply because one has a great deal of money, this does not ensure the validity of his or her stance on politics, relationships, education, or any other matter.

3.15 ARGUMENTUM AD MISERICORDIAM

The argumentum ad misericordiam is also known as the *appeal to pity*. It is an argument that appeals to emotions rather than providing solid evidence or facts to support its claim. By evoking pity, the arguer hopes to persuade the audience or listener to accept his or her conclusion. For example:

Example 1:

Boyfriend: You shouldn't break up with me.

Girlfriend: Why?

Boyfriend: Because the thought of losing you hurts so much.

In this example, the boyfriend is trying to evoke a sense of pity in his girlfriend in order that she might stay with him. However, this is not a logical reason for staying with someone. Simply feeling sorry for another is no reason to agree with his/her claim. Consider these examples:

Example 2:

Come on, I need you to lie for me. If you don't, I will lose my job, my wife, and my kids.

Example 3:

Sue: Let's go to the philosophy lecture on Monday night.

Brad: I cannot go; I have homework.

Sue: If you don't go, I'll have to walk home alone in the dark. Are you sure you won't go?

Example 4:

Professor Dreyfus, please reconsider the grade you gave me on my final. If I don't get an "A," then I won't be able to get into graduate school and my life will be ruined.

In these examples, appeals to pity are made. Rather than providing good reasons in support of the claims, the arguer tries to arouse an emotional response. The ad misericordiam argument is often quite effective. However, we must be careful not to allow emotional responses to replace clear and coherent reasoning.

Chapter Four

Fallacies with Built-In Assumptions

4.1 PETITIO PRINCIPII

This fallacy is sometimes known as *begging the question.* From the Latin, petitio principii is translated as "appealing to the first principles." Petitio principii uses part of its conclusion in its own premise as support. This is a type of circular reasoning. Often this fallacy occurs when one uses two different words—one in the premises and one in the conclusion—which share the same definition. For example:

Example 1:

Abortion is wrong because abortion is unethical.

In this example, the conclusion (abortion is wrong) is supported by the premise (abortion is unethical). However, this argument begs the question because an act that is unethical, by definition, is an act that is wrong. Consider these examples:

Example 2:

Your honor, the defendant should be held responsible for stealing my client's purse because he took something that did not belong to him.

Example 3:

The Bible is true because it contains no falsehoods.

In these examples the conclusions are simply different versions of the premises. The conclusion should be established and supported by the premises; it should not simply be a restatement or variation of them.

4.2 COMPLEX QUESTION

The complex question is not an argument; it is a particular type of question. More specifically, it is a *loaded question*; that is, a question with a built-in assumption. The complex question can often throw off the listener by forcing him or her to answer a flawed question. For example:

Example 1:

Lawyer to defendant: Where did you hide the murder weapon?

This example assumes the defendant knows where the weapon is. If the defendant answers that he did not hide the murder weapon, then the judge and the jury might assume he did have the weapon in his possession at some time. (In legal terms this is referred to as *leading the witness*.) The only way around this question is for the defendant to call to attention that the question is loaded. Consider these additional examples:

Example 2:

When did you stop beating your wife?

Example 3:

When are you going to have children?

In example 2, the assumption is made that the person questioned did abuse his wife. In example 3, the question assumes the individual has decided to have children. The best response to these types of questions is not simply to answer the question as it has been posed. Rather, one should bring to light that the question has built-in assumptions, lest one fall into the trap set by the questioner. Consider the built-in assumptions in the following examples.

Example 4:

How many drinks have you had tonight?

Example 5:

> How much did you enjoy the movie?

We must be careful to avoid asking loaded questions, and we must work to create straightforward, clear dialogue.

4.3 APPEAL TO HUMAN NATURE

This fallacy is an error in reasoning that appeals to "human nature" without clearly defining it. More specifically, it occurs when one uses this vague notion as justification for a particular human action. For example:

Example 1:

> Well of course people worship celebrities—it's our nature to worship them!

Example 2:

> Defendant: Your honor, it's a dog-eat-dog world out there and I was doing what human nature is best at—defending and protecting myself! How can you hold someone responsible for their nature?

Example 3:

> Humans by their very nature are political animals. Thus, it is clear all individuals should participate in the political process.

It is important to remember the appeal to human nature is often used as an excuse for certain behavior. The argument usually claims one should not be held responsible because an action was simply in his or her "human nature." One problem with this kind of appeal is that the notion of human nature itself is unclear. Many people speak of the nature of human beings, but on closer inspection it is difficult to specifically and clearly state what this means and what specific actions fall into this category. Furthermore, even if we were able to arrive at a universal definition, it would not necessarily mean human nature could be used as a license for any type of behavior.

4.4 IS-OUGHT FALLACY

This fallacy occurs when an argument uses a purely descriptive statement (an "is" statement) as a premise and moves to a prescriptive statement (an "ought" statement) as its conclusion. The words "is" and "ought" do not necessarily need to be in the argument for the is-ought fallacy to occur. There will, however, always be a description followed by a prescription. The is-ought fallacy has the following form:

Premise: Descriptive statement ("is").

Conclusion: Prescriptive statement ("ought").

Here are some examples:

Example 1:

Humans have carnivorous teeth. Therefore, you should eat meat.

Example 2:

The phone is on sale. Therefore, you should buy it!

Example 3:

She asked you out. You should go out with her.

As we can see from these examples, the is-ought fallacy usually is found when someone is trying to convince another person to act a certain way. However, we cannot assume we can determine how things *ought* to be, just because we know how things *are*. To do so is flawed reasoning, because a prescriptive suggestion or command cannot be derived solely from a descriptive statement or observation. In other words, just because we have the facts, this does not necessarily mean we always know how others—or ourselves for that matter—should behave because of these facts.

It should be noted that this fallacy, unlike others, is debated by many philosophers. Some intellectuals like John Searle, maintain the is-ought fallacy is not truly a fallacy, but a coherent and valid form of reasoning.[1] I will leave it to the reader to decide whether he or she believes the is-ought fallacy is indeed a fallacy or not.

4.5 PROJECTION

The fallacy of projection occurs when one "projects" personal feelings, beliefs, or attitudes onto another person without evidence to support this assumption. This is similar to the concept of projection found in certain psychological theories. Sigmund Freud believed individuals often project unconscious desires and fears onto the external world. The fallacy of projection is different in that it is more generally applied to lazy assumptions we all sometimes make about others. Projection can easily be described as assuming others' experiences of reality and/or conclusions concerning reality are the same as one's own. For example:

Example 1:

> Of course Sharon will agree with us. She witnessed the attack also. Therefore, even though she is not here to cast a vote, I am sure she will confirm our decision to go to war.

Example 2:

> How can you possibly eat more than one piece of pizza? One piece always fills me up.

Example 3:

> Jonathan is late to work again this morning. I am only late to work when I party the night before. Jonathan must have had a great time partying last night!

Example 4:

> I can see God's handiwork clearly in nature. Anyone who looks at creation will surely come to the same conclusion.

In these examples one projects onto others one's personal beliefs, which have been derived from his or her individual experience. The problem with this type of reasoning is that individuals have different understandings of events, food, other people, nature, and of almost everything else in life. This does not mean that others' interpretations will always be different than one's own. In fact, many people share very similar experiences and interpretations. But, the key point to remember about the fallacy of projection is this: simply because one has arrived at a certain conclusion, it does not follow others will make the same judgment.

4.6 APPEAL TO ANECDOTAL EVIDENCE

An anecdote often refers to a personal experience or a short account of an incident. The fallacy of appealing to anecdotal evidence is usually an argument where one calls upon a personal experience or a passed-down story, then assumes all other like cases will be similar. In this way, it is somewhat like the fallacy of projection. However, the fallacy of anecdotal evidence relies on causal evidence, usually uncorroborated and not necessarily a projection of the individual making the argument. Usually the appeal to anecdotal evidence relies on one specific, exceptional case, and then overgeneralizes from that case. For example:

Example 1:

> Many believe smoking cigarettes causes cancer. This isn't true. My grandmother smoked cigarettes until she was 92 years old, and she did not have cancer.

Example 2:

> How do I know Bigfoot exists? Because I watched a video online where a hunter in Alaska personally encountered Bigfoot!

Example 3:

> Eating at Ricardo's Restaurant will make you sick. How do I know this? Because my uncle ate there last year and the very next day came down with food poisoning.

In these examples, personal incidences are used as premises, and the conclusions are drawn only from these. As critical thinkers, we must consider various accounts in order to arrive at solid conclusions. The limited experience of one or even a small group of people does not provide enough evidence for a guaranteed conclusion. It should be noted that the first example is also the fallacy of the exception disproves the rule.

4.7 NARCISSIST FALLACY

In Greek mythology Narcissus was a young man who was in love with his own image. Narcissism usually refers to a type of behavior that is egotistical or vain. The narcissist fallacy occurs when one assumes others are thinking about them. This is similar to the fallacy of projection, where one projects one's beliefs, values, or feelings onto others. The key difference between these two fallacies, however, is that you commit the narcissist fallacy when you make the false assumption that people notice you, care about you, or are thinking about you. Consider these examples:

Example 1:

> He smiled when I walked by. He must think these new jeans look really good on me.

Example 2:

> My neighbor doesn't talk to me anymore. It's probably because he's jealous of my new car.

Example 3:

> I'll go ahead and pull onto the freeway. Other drivers will see me and let me merge.

Example 4:

> Today the mailman was rude to me and so was the toll booth attendant. I can't believe people have been treating me so poorly on my birthday!

In each of these examples an assumption is made about others and their motivations and concerns. If we are honest with ourselves, we know those who we encounter in everyday life are not necessarily thinking about us, even when they treat us in a certain manner. Other people have their own personal preoccupations—financial, marital, political, medical, spiritual, and so on—which often do not include us.

4.8 ANTHROPOMORPHISM

This fallacy gets its name from two Greek words: *anthropos*, meaning human, and *morphe*, meaning form. This fallacy occurs when one assumes a non-human being or thing has the same characteristics as a human. Often this involves a projection of human emotions or behavior onto something non-human. For example:

Example 1:

> Because of our lack of respect for nature, the earth has become angry with us humans.

Example 2:

> As I look at the magnificent California redwoods, I feel them calling my name and extending their love to me.

Example 3:

> Don't leave your laptop in the direct sunlight. Computers get stubborn and vengeful if they overheat.

In these examples, human emotions or attributes are assumed to be part of the non-human world. We must be honest with ourselves and try to recognize projection of this sort. When we allow ourselves to make unfounded assumptions about nature and non-human creatures, we are reasoning with inauthenticity, laziness, and presumption. May our reasoning, instead, be built with the principles of critical thinking, which will help us avoid anthropomorphism and other fallacies.

4.9 FALLACY OF EFFICIENCY

Many people value efficiency in various areas of life — business, school, technology, travel — and this is understandable. Often, if something is quicker, more effective, or practical, then it is seen as necessarily better than that which is considered less efficient. However, we should remember that simply because a person, action, or event is more efficient, this does not always mean it is superior. To make this assumption is to commit the fallacy of efficiency. Consider these examples:

Example 1:

Jessica: You should buy the latest phone, it's really fast.

Bert: I am quite satisfied with my phone. It works fine and it is simple to use.

Jessica: I can't believe you, Bert. Your phone is old and slow. Faster is always better!

Example 2:

Doris: You should take Highway 5 to Santa Barbara; it is the quickest route.

Stanley: I prefer to take Highway 1. It may take longer, but the view of the ocean is spectacular.

Doris: Sounds like a waste of time and gas.

Example 3:

College student: I have decided to major in philosophy. I love reading Plato, Aristotle, Kant, and other influential thinkers in Western history.

Mother: What job will that prepare you for? You should major in business. A business degree is the only way to quickly secure a job after college.

We hear conversations like this regularly. However, neither the correctness of one's decisions nor the quality of one's life depend solely on speed, effectiveness, or practicality. Consider aged wine, a meal made from scratch, or music, art, and literature. Many of the things in life we treasure and appreciate are not practical or efficient at all.

4.10 THE EXCEPTION DISPROVES THE RULE

This fallacy occurs when one assumes an exception disproves a well-established rule or acts as a substantial refutation to the rule. While an exception may prove there are indeed deviations, this does not guarantee that a well-substantiated general rule is absent. Consider these common examples:

Example 1:

Professor of ethics: Generally speaking, human beings have always found cannibalism reprehensible and morally unacceptable.

Student: That is not true. I read about a tribe in New Guinea that eats their dead!

Example 2:

Jodie: The rule of law, in various forms, has been paramount in all organized civilizations.

Belinda: You are incorrect. I recently watched a documentary about a commune in the Southwest without laws.

Example 3:

Doctor: Usually, antibiotics help stop bacterial infections. I recommend you take antibiotics.

Patient: Antibiotics don't work. My aunt had a bacterial infection and antibiotics didn't help her.

While the detractors, in each of these cases, may be correct with their specific examples, the exception does not invalidate the general rule of thumb. In fact, the sheer rarity of the exception can actually reinforce the rule itself. We must remember that simply because there is an example that demonstrates an exception, this does not always constitute a refutation.

4.11 SUBJECTIVIST FALLACY

Today it is quite common to hear the phrase, "That may be true for you, but it is not true for me." This is the quintessential subjectivist fallacy. This fallacy is called the subjectivist fallacy because many who use this erroneous type of argument mistakenly believe that all truth ultimately depends on the subject or the individual. This fallacy rests on a misunderstanding of what constitutes truth, confusing or conflating truth with belief.

It is critical that we distinguish between belief and truth. If something is true, then it describes accurately the way things are. As philosopher J. L. Mackie explains: "If we do take statements to be the primary bearers of truth, there seems to be a very simple answer to the question, what is it for them to be true: for a statement to be true is for things to be as they are stated to be."[2]

In contrast to truth, a belief is an opinion or conviction about something. A belief can be true or false. For example, if a person believes that 2 + 2 = 7, then he or she believes a falsehood, not a truth. Simply because one believes something, this does not make their belief accurate.

Also, it is important to distinguish between truth and taste or preference. Someone might prefer Nietzsche's writings to Plato's. This is merely a matter of preference, not of truth. Or, someone might like the taste of tea over coffee. Again, this is simply one's taste; this is not an issue of truth or falsehood.

The subjectivist fallacy is quite commonly used as a mechanism for avoiding taking seriously the views and opinions of others. As critical thinkers, we should not take this easy method of escape. The beliefs and arguments of others should be considered in a serious and analytical manner, and they should be viewed from a standpoint that understands the vital difference between truth and belief.

NOTES

1. Searle, John. "How to Derive 'Ought' from 'Is,'" in *Philosophical Review*, 1964. 73: 43–58.
2. Mackie, J.L. *Truth, Probability and Paradox: Studies in Philosophical Logic*. Oxford: Clarendon Press, 1972. p. 22.

Chapter Five

Causal Fallacies

5.1 FALLACY OF THE FALSE CAUSE

The fallacy of the false cause is an argument that assumes there is a causal relation between two events, without providing supporting evidence. Events often occur simultaneously or consecutively, however, this does not mean they are necessarily related. For example:

Example 1:

> The Chinese restaurant was robbed Friday night and again Saturday night. It must have been robbed by the same perpetrator.

Example 2:

> Floods and tornadoes devastated the small town of Green Hills. It is clear a Divine Being was punishing the town for its non-religious practices.

In the first example, the assumption is made that due to the same location of the robberies, the cause of both crimes must be the same. Without further supporting information, however, it is impossible to know if the same criminal was responsible for both events. In the second example, the assumption is made that two consecutive events (the town's non-religious practices and the floods and tornadoes) are causally related. But, like the first example, a causal relationship cannot be established.

All causal fallacies rest on a misunderstanding of cause and effect. The clearest examples of these are the fallacy of the false cause (above), the fallacy of the single cause, post hoc ergo propter hoc, and the slippery slope fallacy. These last three arguments will be explained next, followed by the gambler's fallacy and the appeal to consequences.

5.2 FALLACY OF THE SINGLE CAUSE

This fallacy is very similar to the fallacy of the false cause, described above. In fact, some consider it to be a version of the false cause. The fallacy of the single cause, however, states an event has only one root or reason, when in fact there may be multiple causes. In contrast, the false cause fallacy is erroneous in its assumption of the cause in general. Consider this example of the fallacy of the single cause:

Example 1:

> Mr. Williams gunned down three innocent people because he was on drugs.

According to this claim, the cause of the shooting was drugs. However, situations like this are usually multifaceted and complicated. It is highly doubtful drugs were the sole cause of Mr. Williams' crime; drugs were most likely only one causal component of the complex event. Drugs combined with anger, fear, exhaustion, desperation, and/or ignorance might be a more accurate explanation. In any case, we simply do not know all of the causal factors involved in this case, so we need to refrain from assuming only one cause. Consider the following example:

Example 2:

> There is a simple explanation as to why the terrorists attacked us: they hate us.

In this argument, the stated conclusion is clearly an oversimplification. Hatred may or may not be one causal factor among several, but many other explanations should be considered when discussing terrorism. We must always remember that events often have more than one causal component.

5.3 POST HOC ERGO PROPTER HOC

Another fallacy of causation, the name of this fallacy translates from the Latin as "after this, therefore because of this." It is also known simply as the *post hoc fallacy*. This fallacy occurs when one presumes that two consecutive, but independently occurring events, are causally related. In other words, one assumes that because one event happened after another event, the first event must have caused the second. For example:

Example 1:

Smith was elected Governor in May. In June, crime rates skyrocketed. Clearly, Smith must have caused crime to increase.

Example 2:

I lost my wallet the afternoon after I kicked my neighbor's cat. Therefore, my unethical act caused me somehow to lose my wallet.

Example 3:

My favorite team won after I prayed for a victory. Therefore, prayer works.

Like the fallacy of the false cause and the fallacy of the single cause, the post hoc fallacy rests on a misunderstanding of cause and effect. Remember, simply because two events occur sequentially, we cannot infer the former event necessarily caused the latter. We must be careful not to project a causal relationship onto unrelated events.

5.4 SLIPPERY SLOPE

This fallacy occurs when one erroneously argues that if a certain act or event takes place, it will necessarily lead to a chain of events, ending in a dramatic or disastrous final result. The slippery slope is a fallacy precisely because we can never know if a whole series of events and/or a certain result is determined to follow one event or action in particular. Usually, but not always, the slippery slope argument is used as a fear tactic. Consider these examples:

Example 1:

You should not major in philosophy. If you do, you'll never get a good job, you'll lose friends, and no one will want to marry you. If you major in philosophy, you'll end up penniless and alone.

Example 2:

Playing the lottery will lead to gambling addiction, which means losing your house, your spouse, and everything that is precious to you. You'll find yourself homeless on the streets of Las Vegas, begging for change.

Example 3:

Marijuana is the gateway drug. Using it will lead to cocaine, heroin, and crack use. Smoke a joint, and before you know it, you'll find yourself with an unquenchable desire for crack!

As we can see from these examples, the slippery slope fallacy claims to know the precise causal links and result following a certain event or action. Furthermore, these events usually end in a negative result. Yet the slippery slope fallacy can also argue for a chain of causal events that necessarily lead to a positive result. For example:

Example 4:

Advertisement: Call now and purchase your own Hollywood Complete Home Gym System! Once it arrives, you'll be able to work out every day, gaining energy, losing weight, and finally being in control of your life! By making the phone call today, you'll be strong and sexy in just a few months!

With this example, it becomes clear the slippery slope can end in one of two extreme places: positive or negative. It should be noted, however, the slippery slope always leads to a dramatic result, and always implies the series of events leading to that result necessarily followed from the first action or event. Sometimes, a slippery slope fallacy does not include or explain the linking events between the first and final ones. For example:

Example 5:

If Barbara rents her house to college students, the property value of the entire neighborhood will drop.

Example 6:

If we allow the government to listen to our phone calls, then before we know it, even our sex lives will be monitored!

These two examples are slightly different versions of the slippery slope fallacy. They both follow the same pattern as presented above, but with the implicit assumption of negative causal events, rather than a clear presentation of a chain of events.

5.5 GAMBLER'S FALLACY

This fallacy of causation occurs when one mistakenly believes an independently occurring event, such as a coin toss, has a causal effect on a separate event, such as a second coin toss. It is named the gambler's fallacy because this type of reasoning is commonly (but not exclusively) found in casinos. For example, if a person wins three hands of cards in a row, he or she might think, "I am on a roll! I am sure to continue winning!" However, there is not a causal relationship between previous card games and later card games—they are separate and non-causally related. Consider these examples:

Example 1:

> I bought three lottery tickets and the first two were winners! I am sure to win on the third ticket, too!

Example 2:

> The Raiders won the last two Monday nights. We can safely assume they will win next Monday night as well.

As seen in the above examples, the gambler's fallacy is often used to predict an upcoming event will be the same as a previous event. However, it is also commonly used to predict the opposite result. Here are some examples:

Example 3:

> Our first two children were boys. This means our next child will certainly be a girl.

Example 4:

> I am sure the Lakers will win their next game. How can I know this? Because they have lost five games in a row and they have to break their losing streak soon.

The fact that this fallacy can be used to predict opposite results makes its flawed nature glaringly evident. Yet the central issue here is this: the gambler's fallacy, like other causal fallacies, confuses the notion of cause and effect. One must remember that there are two types of events: causal and non-causal. A causal event is one in which an action or event necessarily causes a following event, such as a pool cue hitting a billiard ball, causing the ball to roll. A non-causal event is one that has no necessary or predictable following event, such as a winning raffle ticket foretelling future wins or losses.

5.6 APPEAL TO CONSEQUENCES

The appeal to consequences is a causal fallacy stating that the truth of a proposition is determined by the negative or positive consequences of that proposition. In other words, this fallacy is committed when one argues a statement must be true or false, depending on whether the consequences are perceived to be good or bad. For example:

Example 1:

Howard: I know God does not exist.

Susan: What evidence do you have to support this claim?

Howard: Well, just look at all the harm that has been done in the name of God!

In this example, Howard does not provide solid premises to support his claim. Instead he points out that belief in God has had certain negative consequences. However, simply because harm has been done in the name of God, this does not mean God does not exist. Likewise, simply because some churches and other religious institutions feed, clothe, and provide shelter for the poor, this does not necessarily mean their religious beliefs are grounded in reality. Consider these examples:

Example 2:

Evolutionary theory is correct for many reasons. The strongest evidence for evolution lies in the fact that people who accept this theory are more civilized than those who do not.

Example 3:

I do not believe that corporate media would present false information simply to gain higher ratings. The thought of this is so disturbing and depressing it cannot possibly be true.

In each of these examples the arguer appeals to the consequences of a particular belief in order to accept or dismiss it. The problem with this type of reasoning is that there is not a causal relationship between the entailments and the truth of a proposition. Consequences often have nothing to do with the truth or falsity of their cause.

Chapter Six

Some Non-Western Fallacies

So far, we have considered many logical fallacies and rhetorical techniques originating from the Western intellectual tradition. In the non-Western world, such as India and China, logic has also played a central and foundational role. When studying these traditions, it is fascinating to see that many logical rules, definitions, and systems share far more similarities than dissimilarities with the West, leading one to question the distinction between Western and non-Western logic. In the following, we will look at six logical fallacies from the *Nyāya-sūtra*, one of the oldest and most influential logic texts arising from the Asian continent.[1]

6.1 QUIBBLE OVER METAPHOR

This fallacy occurs when one responds to a metaphor as if it were to be taken literally. It is usually employed as a rhetorical device to avoid taking the position or argument of the interlocuter seriously. It is also often used to dismiss the opponents claim or position. For example:

Example 1:

> Doctor to patient: You need to begin listening to your body—don't over-eat, get more sleep, and exercise regularly.
>
> (Six months later)
>
> Doctor to patient: I recommended that you listen to your body, but you continue to live an unhealthy lifestyle.

Patient: I have been listening to my body! It hasn't said a damn word to me!

Example 2:

Albert Einstein once said that religion, art, and science are all branches of the same tree. Einstein was wrong. Religion, art, and science are not natural phenomena like plants and trees.

In the first example, the patient responds to the doctor by interpreting "listen to your body" in a crudely literal way, using this as a pretext for dismissing the doctor's advice. In the second example, Einstein's metaphor is dismissed as false because the interpreter seems to misunderstand the metaphor, by taking it literally. In both cases, the metaphor is misinterpreted, leading to an erroneous conclusion, which is precisely the quibble over metaphor.

6.2 QUIBBLE OVER TERM

The fallacy of quibbling over term is quite similar to the fallacy of equivocation. It involves taking a term used by one's opponent and interpreting it in a way which makes the opponent's argument seem faulty. For example:

You said you will fight for freedom; however, you also argue that people should not be free to smoke cigarettes indoors. You obviously don't believe in freedom. You have contradicted yourself and your claim cannot be taken seriously.

As in the fallacy of equivocation, a term is used in two different senses to make an argument. "Freedom" is used both in a general way and in a specific, restrictive sense. By utilizing both meanings of the term, the arguer tries to dismiss his opponent's position.

6.3 FALLACY OF CONTRADICTION

A contradiction occurs when two statements cannot simultaneously be true. For example, if one states that she is currently pregnant, and also that she is not currently pregnant, this is a contradiction. The fallacy of contradiction is not difficult to understand. It occurs when one contradicts oneself in an argument or in a response to a question. For example:

Example 1:

Judge: Were you at your home address the night the crime occurred?

Defendant: No. I was not at my home address the night it occurred, but I did quickly stop by to pick up my wallet.

Example 2:

Juliette: Did you pass the philosophy class?

Alex: I did pass the philosophy class. Well, I would have passed if I didn't withdraw first.

Example 3:

Knowledge is fleeting and uncertain. In the final analysis, no one can know anything.

In the first two examples, the respondent contradicts his or her own previous statement. This demonstrates that they may not be reliable or may be intentionally avoiding the question. In the third example, a contradiction is also present: if no one can know anything, then one would not be able to know that one knows nothing. It should also be noted that the fallacy of contradiction is quite similar to the law of non-contradiction, an axiomatic principle in the Western philosophical tradition.

6.4 FALLACY OF THE UNPROVED

This fallacy occurs when one relies on an unproven premise, and then argues for a conclusion based on that premise. In essence, it is an argument that relies on a statement which purports to be a fact but is unverified. For example:

Example 1:

Premise: The biblical account states Jesus was resurrected from the dead.

Premise: Since Jesus was resurrected from the dead, this indicates immortality is possible.

Conclusion: Immortality is possible.

In this example, the argument rests on an unproven premise: the account of Jesus' resurrection. From this unproven premise, the arguer goes on to draw his conclusion. While this may be convincing for some believers, for others this argument is flawed due to its unproven premise. In order for the argument to be more convincing, the arguer should have demonstrated the proof of his premise first. Here is a different example of the fallacy of the unproved:

Example 2:

> College is a guaranteed door to financial success. Therefore, all young people should work toward a college degree.

Here, the conclusion that all young people should work toward a degree, is based on an unproven premise: college guarantees financial success. If one is not careful, one might be persuaded by such an argument. It is vital that we carefully look out for arguments which rest on unproven premises, such as in the fallacy of the unproved.

6.5 INCONCLUSIVE FALLACY

The inconclusive fallacy is similar to the argumentum ad ignorantiam. It consists of an argument which relies on a lack of proof, maintaining the conclusion follows from this lack of proof. However, like the ad ignorantiam fallacy, a lack of proof does not always provide a secure foundation for an argument. Consider these examples:

Example 1:

> Lawyer: There is no evidence my client was at the crime scene; this means he is innocent.

Example 2:

> Husband: You cannot prove I cheated on you; therefore, I did not cheat.

In each of these cases, the conclusion rests on a *lack of proof as evidence.* However, simply because there is no evidence the client was at the crime scene, or the husband is an adulterer, it does not follow they are innocent. This is precisely the flaw: this fallacy uses inconclusive evidence as if it were able to prove something conclusive.

6.6 DEVIANT FALLACY

This fallacy is similar to the fallacy of composition. It argues that since a limited number of parts have a certain characteristic, the whole (to which the parts belong) must share the same characteristic. Consider these examples of the deviant fallacy:

Example 1:

> If one reads about the crusades in the Middle Ages, one will see that religion is the source of war. This is why I reject all religion: it causes violence, war, and death.

Example 2:

> The last time I voted for a Green Party candidate, he turned out to be involved in money laundering. From this experience, I have concluded that all Green Party politicians are dishonest.

In the first example, the assumption is made that all religions cause violence and war. While various world religions have certainly been involved in conflicts throughout the ages, there are countless examples of religious institutions and individuals who opposed war, promoting peaceful and progressive causes, and advocating nonviolence and equal rights. Consider Mahatma Gandhi; Martin Luther King, Jr.; Dorothy Day; the Dalai Lama; and Desmond Tutu to name a few.

In the second example, the supposition is made that all Green Party politicians are alike: corrupt. However, simply because some are crooked, it does not follow that all are. In both cases, like the fallacy of composition, the arguer makes a sweeping generalization about the whole from a limited experience of the parts.

In both Western and non-Western logic, well-constructed arguments should avoid equivocation, contradictions, lack of proof, assumptions, and over-generalizations. By avoiding these pitfalls, one will be more likely to formulate valid and strong arguments.

NOTES

1. Information in this chapter is primarily taken from the following sources: (1) *The Nyāya-sūtra: Selections with Early Commentaries*. Translated by Matthew Dasti and Stephen Phillips. Cambridge: Hackett, 2017. (2) *The Nyāya-Sūtras of Gotama*. Translated by Vidyabhusana. New York: AMS Press, 1974. (3) *Inference and Fallacies Discussed in Ancient Indian Logic (with special reference to Nyāya and Buddhism)*. Pradeep P. Gokhale. Delhi: Sri Satguru Publications, 1992. (4) *The Character of Logic in India*. B.K. Matilal. Albany: State University of New York Press, 1998.

Chapter Seven

Valid and Invalid Argument Forms

So far, we have discussed many logical fallacies in this book. Now we will learn how to recognize and utilize good reasoning by introducing five traditional valid argument forms and two traditional invalid argument forms. For centuries, logicians and scientists have used these forms as templates for structuring arguments. The five valid forms are: modus ponens, modus tollens, disjunctive syllogism, hypothetical syllogism, and constructive dilemma. The two invalid forms are the fallacy of denying the antecedent and the fallacy of affirming the consequent. Familiarity with these arguments is essential in the study of logic. They should be learned and remembered as prototypes of valid argumentation.

7.1 MODUS PONENS

Modus ponens is made up of two premises and a conclusion. It begins with a conditional statement as its first premise. A conditional statement is an "if-then" statement. For example: "If I drop the cup of coffee then it will spill." The "if" component is called the antecedent ("If I drop the cup of coffee . . ."), and the "then" component is called the consequent (". . . then it will spill"). The second premise of modus ponens always affirms the antecedent of the conditional statement. For example:

If the printer prints in color, then it is out of black ink. (First premise)

The printer is printing in color. (Second premise)

Therefore, the printer is out of black ink. (Conclusion)

In this example, we see clearly that the antecedent of the first premise is affirmed in the second premise. In the conclusion, we see another characteristic always found in modus ponens: the consequent of the conditional premise is affirmed. In fact, modus ponens is translated from the Latin as the "mode of affirming." In symbolic form, modus ponens looks like this:

If A then B.

A.

Therefore, B.

Modus ponens always follows this pattern. Here are some more examples of modus ponens.

Example 1:

If Bertrand Russell was a philosopher then he was an intellectual.

Bertrand Russell was a philosopher.

Therefore, Bertrand Russell was an intellectual.

Example 2:

If Mr. Jones murdered the bank teller in the botched robbery, then Mr. Jones is guilty and should be punished.

According to the video evidence, Mr. Jones did murder the bank teller in the botched robbery.

So, Mr. Jones is guilty and should be punished.

Example 3:

If I see the chef sneeze into the spaghetti, then I will not eat it.

I see the chef sneezing into the spaghetti.

I will not eat the spaghetti.

In all of these examples, one can clearly see the form of modus ponens. We should memorize this valid argument form and use it as a guide for structuring our own arguments.

7.2 MODUS TOLLENS

This valid argument form is similar to modus ponens. However, where modus ponens affirms the antecedent of the conditional statement, modus tollens denies the consequent of the conditional statement. This is why it is translated from the Latin as the "mode of removing." For example:

If the candle is lit, then there is a flame.

There is no flame.

Therefore, the candle is not lit.

Here, the consequent of the conditional statement is denied (or negated) in the second premise. And from this, it logically follows that the conclusion is true. Modus tollens takes the following symbolic form:

If A then B.

Not B.

Therefore, not A.

Here are some more examples of modus tollens:

Example 1:

If Steven was born in the United States, then he is a citizen of the United States.

Steven is not a citizen of the United States.

Therefore, Steven was not born in the United States.

Example 2:

If Sally has a cat, then she is a pet owner.

Sally is not a pet owner.

Therefore, Sally does not have a cat.

Example 3:

If the magician's assistant had been decapitated, then she would be dead.

The magician's assistant is not dead.

Therefore, the magician's assistant was not decapitated.

In these examples we see clearly the modus tollens pattern. Modus tollens, like modus ponens, is a valid and coherent logical form that should be remembered and employed.

7.3 DISJUNCTIVE SYLLOGISM

The disjunctive syllogism is perhaps the easiest valid form to remember. This form always has a disjunctive statement—an "either/or" statement—as one of its premises. For example:

Either Bach wrote Mass in B Minor or Wagner wrote it.

Wagner did not write Mass in B Minor.

Therefore, Bach wrote Mass in B Minor.

In the above, we are presented with two options in the first premise: Bach or Wagner. If these really are the only two choices, and if Wagner did not write Mass in B Minor, then the conclusion follows logically from the premises. If there were other choices that were intentionally left out, then this would be the fallacy of bifurcation.

Here we are reminded that all valid argument forms rest on the assumption that the premises are true. That is, the forms provide the structure for valid arguments, but in reality, the content of the forms may or may not be true. For the sake of learning the traditional argument forms and how to create good arguments, we will take the examples herein at face value. And, on this assumption, the above argument is valid.

The disjunctive syllogism has the following symbolic form:

Either A or B.

Not B (or, not A).

Therefore, A (or, B).

From this symbolic form we can clearly see that it does not matter which side of the disjunctive statement is denied. If one option is negated, then the other must be true. Consider these examples.

Example 1:

Either Holmes solved the crime or Dr. Watson solved the crime.

Dr. Watson did not solve the crime.

Therefore, Holmes solved the crime.

Example 2:

Either you go to college or you get a job.

You did not get a job.

So, you will go to college.

Example 3:

Truth is either a construct of institutions or it is the correspondence of language to reality.

Truth is not a construct of institutions.

Therefore, truth is the correspondence of language to reality.

The disjunctive syllogism is a valid form of reasoning when there are only two options to choose from. If possible, when creating good arguments, we should try to use forms like the disjunctive syllogism.

7.4 HYPOTHETICAL SYLLOGISM

The hypothetical syllogism is made up of three conditional statements: one in each of the two premises and one in the conclusion. This is also known as the chain argument because it links together all components of the premises and conclusion. For example:

If I move to the Bay Area, then I will need an income.

If I need an income, then I will need a job.

So, if I move to the Bay Area, then I will need a job.

The symbolic form of the hypothetical syllogism is as follows:

If A then B.

If B then C.

So, if A then C.

This argument form is quite easy to recognize because it consists entirely of conditional statements. Like the other valid argument forms, the hypothetical syllogism always provides an argument with good structure, but not necessarily true content. For the purpose of illustrating the hypothetical syllogism, we will assume the premises are true in the following three final examples of this form.

Example 1:

If community colleges continue to cut classes, then fewer Americans will have access to education.

If fewer Americans have access to education, then poverty will increase.

Therefore, if community colleges continue to cut classes, poverty will increase.

Example 2:

If I rob the bank, then I may kill someone.

If I kill someone, then there is a possibility I will spend my life in prison.

So, if I rob the bank, then there is a possibility I will spend my life in prison.

Example 3:

If the atheists are correct, then there is no God.

If there is no God, then intelligent design is false.

Therefore, if the atheists are correct, then intelligent design is false.

7.5 CONSTRUCTIVE DILEMMA

This is the final of the five valid argument forms we will discuss. The constructive dilemma uses both disjunctive and conditional statements. It also is the only valid argument form that uses three premises instead of two. Here is an example:

We will either rent or buy a home.

If we rent, then we will need to move.

If we buy, then we will stay.

So, we will either move or we will stay.

The symbolic form of this constructive dilemma is as follows:

Either A or B.

If A then C.

If B then D.

So, either C or D.

Here we see that the constructive dilemma begins with a disjunctive statement as its first premise. In the second and third premises, it contains conditional statements. Finally, it concludes with a disjunctive statement that affirms the consequents of the second and third premises. Here are some more examples of the constructive dilemma:

Example 1:

Either we celebrate Hanukkah, or we celebrate Christmas.

If we celebrate Hanukkah, then we will drive to Los Angeles.

If we celebrate Christmas, then we will drive to San Francisco.

Therefore, we will either drive to Los Angeles or to San Francisco.

Example 2:

Humans either have instrumental value or intrinsic value.

If humans have instrumental value, then their worth is measured by their efficiency.

If humans have intrinsic value, then they have worth regardless of how efficient they are.

So, either human worth is measured by efficiency or humans have worth regardless of their efficiency.

Example 3:

Either Sigmund Freud was correct, or C.S. Lewis was correct.

If Sigmund Freud was correct, then the idea of God is simply a projection of unconscious desires.

If C.S. Lewis was correct, then the theism of the Bible is true, and God exists independently of our unconscious desires.

So, either God is a projection of our unconscious desires, or God exists independently of our unconscious desires.

In these examples, we clearly see the constructive dilemma employed. It is an especially helpful argument form to use when making plans in everyday life, or when debating abstract theories.

Like the other four valid argument forms we have discussed, the constructive dilemma is simply a template to be used when creating good arguments. Of course, it is not always possible to use one of these five forms. However, they are vital to the study of logic, and useful when one is seeking solid argument structure.

7.6 FALLACY OF DENYING THE ANTECEDENT

Now that we have discussed five traditional valid argument forms, we will look at two common invalid argument forms. We should remember that a formal fallacy is an argument containing an error in its structure. Both the fallacy of denying the antecedent and the fallacy of affirming the consequent are formal fallacies. Let's consider the first:

If I am patient, then I will find a job.

I am not patient.

Therefore, I will not find a job.

Here is the symbolic form of the argument:

If A, then B

Not A.

Therefore, not B.

We see in this example that the antecedent in the first premise is denied in the second premise. This denial leads to a denial of the consequent in the conclusion. However, this argument is fallacious. Simply because the person is impatient does not necessarily mean he or she will not find a job. Here are some additional examples:

Example 1:

If Aquinas was a rationalist, then he believed in a spiritual realm.

Aquinas was not a rationalist.

Therefore, Aquinas did not believe in a spiritual realm.

Example 2:

If Franklin is guilty of murder, then he should be incarcerated.

Franklin is not guilty of murder.

Therefore, he should not be incarcerated.

Example 3:

If the engine runs on diesel, then it will have a long life.

The engine is a gas engine, not a diesel.

Therefore, it will not have a long life.

It is clear from these examples that a denied antecedent does not necessarily lead to a false consequent. It should be noted that if an argument takes the form of the fallacy of denying the antecedent, it is always invalid.

7.7 FALLACY OF AFFIRMING THE CONSEQUENT

Like the previous formal fallacy, this fallacy is structurally invalid. Known as the fallacy of affirming the consequent, it takes the following form:

If Sandy loses her job, then she will not be able to pay her rent.

Sandy is not able to pay her rent.

Sandy must have lost her job.

In symbolic form:

If A, then B.

B.

Therefore, A.

As seen in the structure of the argument, the consequent of the first premise is affirmed in the second premise, leading to an affirmation of the antecedent in the conclusion. Sometimes this fallacy is known as "reasoning in reverse." Consider these examples:

Example 1:

If Barbara believes in karma, then she will act responsibly.

Barbara acts responsibly.

Barbara must believe in karma.

Example 2:

If John is a Humean, then he is an empiricist.

John is an empiricist.

Therefore, John is a Humean.

Example 3:

If rent prices increase, then Kevin will be forced to move.

Kevin was forced to move.

Therefore, rent prices must have gone up.

Consider example 2. Even if the reader is not familiar with the terms "Humean" or "empiricist," the reader can be certain the argument is structurally invalid because it takes the form of affirming the consequent.

Both the fallacy of denying the antecedent and the fallacy of affirming the consequent are invalid argument forms which demonstrate how not to argue. One should avoid using these in argumentation, instead formulating arguments in accordance with a valid form such as the five structures discussed earlier in this chapter.

Appendix I

Exercises

PART ONE

Instructions: Create an argument that commits the fallacy listed below. If necessary, provide the context for each of your examples.

1. False dilemma
2. Slippery slope
3. Argumentum ad baculum
4. Argumentum ad hominem, abusive
5. Reductionism
6. Anthropomorphism
7. Tu quoque
8. Equivocation
9. Argumentum ad populum
10. Red herring
11. Shifting the burden of proof
12. Petitio principii
13. Appeal to consequences
14. Complex question
15. Fallacy of composition
16. Fallacy of division
17. False cause
18. Argumentum ad verecundiam
19. Ignoratio elenchi
20. Post hoc ergo propter hoc

PART TWO

Instructions: In the following, identify the informal logical fallacy or fallacies committed.

1. Marriage is just natural. It is a fundamental component of human life and it springs from human nature. To oppose marriage is to oppose human nature.
2. Plato was one of the first great philosophers. Plato taught that democracy was inherently flawed. It follows then, that all philosophers are opposed to democracy, and one should be cautious when reading their works.
3. The day after I broke up with my girlfriend, my car would not start. I am sure she sabotaged my car engine.
4. Why am I supporting candidate Mulhauser for governor? Because Chuck Norris supports him! Chuck Norris is a very successful actor and he must know what he is talking about.
5. Advertisement: This is the new app your phone has been waiting for!
6. Seventy-three percent of all those surveyed outside the Bentonville Thrift-Mart opposed abortion. Therefore, it is safe to say the majority of Americans oppose abortion.
7. I ate breakfast at the Greasy Spoon two years ago. The coffee was terrible. The Greasy Spoon is an awful restaurant.
8. Are you a college student or are you a drop-out?
9. Our new president is secretly a Socialist. How do I know this? Because my uncle Ricardo told me, and my uncle is an honest man.
10. Boss: I need the report by Tuesday. Employee: Why do you need it by Tuesday? Boss: Because if I don't have it on Tuesday, you'll be out of work on Wednesday!
11. Christians say God is love. Love is an emotion. So, God is simply an emotion.
12. Ken argues the Iraq War was morally wrong. But Ken is just bitter because his wife left him. He is just being emotional.
13. Keith: War is always caused by intolerant religious fanatics. Owen: Really? What about the Civil War, World War I, World War II, the Korean War, and the Vietnam War? Keith: Exactly! You have proven my point.
14. After the young man read Richard Dawkins' book *The God Delusion*, he took his own life. It is clear that Dawkins' book caused the man to commit suicide. Furthermore, Dawkins should be held responsible for the young man's death.
15. The Founding Fathers argued that all people are created equal. This is clearly untrue. Some people are better athletes than others; some are

more intelligent than others. So, the Founding Fathers must have been wrong.

16. Either God created the world as stated in the book of Genesis, or life is a product of random chance. Both options cannot be true. If God created the world, then the Bible is true. If God did not create the world, then life is meaningless.
17. Bumper sticker: You can either save the trees or use plastic toilet paper!
18. How big does my butt look in these new jeans?
19. I guarantee you with absolute certainty, if you earn a business degree, you will definitely, in all likelihood, find an excellent, high-paying job.
20. You say you are against war. But I know for a fact that you were previously in the military.

PART THREE

Instructions: In the following, identify the informal logical fallacy or fallacies committed.

1. Animals are not human beings. So, you should not feel guilty when conducting medical experiments on them.
2. Since we cannot come to a universal consensus concerning the definition of pornography, we should reject the entire discussion and move on to a more easily defined topic.
3. Communism is defined as the control of the masses by a fascist dictator who simply wants power and control. In Communist countries people must wait in long lines for food and no one gets health care. Furthermore, the media is censored in those countries. For these reasons I reject Communism.
4. Laws against underage drinking are worthless. Teenagers are going to drink no matter what. It is time we get rid of underage drinking laws.
5. The only reason Professor Clark requires students to buy the book he wrote is so he will make money.
6. I will not vote for a politician from the Bay Area. The last time I voted for a politician from the Bay Area, the economy collapsed!
7. Why should I listen to you when you tell me not to join the Army? You joined the Army when you were eighteen years old!
8. Lawyer: Why did you accept the bribe? Politician: Well, everyone in Washington is a little corrupt.

9. Emma: I was abducted by aliens two years ago. Kristopher: How do know this is true? How can you be sure it wasn't a hallucination or a dream? Emma: Well, prove it isn't true!
10. Professor to students: What do you think? Was Bill Clinton a great president or was he the greatest president?
11. There must be a universal, objective framework for ethics. If not, then everyone would just do whatever they pleased.
12. Crime is either caused by ignorance, a poor economy, or both. If ignorance is the cause, then a good education is the answer. If a poor economy is the cause, then Karl Marx was right, and Capitalism should be replaced by a more just economic system.
13. I spent three years taking college classes and all I ended up with was a bunch of debt. I couldn't even get a decent job afterwards. College is a joke.
14. Nashmin: I believe rape is wrong, and it should carry a life sentence. Randy: Rape has always been a part of human existence. We find examples of it in every society that has ever existed. We even find examples of it in the animal kingdom. It shouldn't carry a life sentence. Nashmin: That is not a good argument. Randy: Well, neither one of us is really right. What is true for you isn't necessarily true for me.
15. Susan: Why should I vote for Senator Clark? Paul: Because everyone knows he is the best candidate.
16. My philosophy professor said religion comes from a deep fear of not being able to explain our natural world. So, religion is bunk.
17. Love is simply a chemical reaction in the brain.
18. Let me clearly define college: the warping of young minds through brainwashing by cultural Marxists.
19. Do you have a minute to help save the planet?
20. Roy: I have decided to leave my wife. Kathy: Why? It seems like you have a solid relationship. Roy: Well, my brother told me my marriage is a sham. He ought to know. He has been married four times.

PART FOUR

Instructions: Identify the fallacy or fallacies committed in the following. If the example does not contain a fallacy, explain.

1. People who believe in God are like little children who believe in Santa Claus and the Tooth Fairy. When will they outgrow these childish beliefs?

2. Tests on Mr. Brown have not found any physical cause for his illness. Therefore, his illness must stem from a psychological disorder.
3. Only Holmes and Watson investigated the crime. Either Holmes or Watson solved the crime. Holmes did not solve the crime. Therefore, Watson must have solved the crime.
4. We conclusively know the Syrian War is immoral, because it is clearly unethical. And, anything that is unethical is certainly wrong.
5. I reject Senator Williams' proposal because he is an idiot!
6. If we really believed in freedom and equal rights, then we would tear down all of the prisons in America. Inmates do not have freedom and equal rights.
7. The new car dealership occasionally has a good sale. If you go there to buy a car, they may or may not be having a sale.
8. It must be an excellent book. It has been on the New York Times bestseller list for ten weeks!
9. Student: What should I do to succeed in your class? Professor: The answer is simple: You need to get an A!
10. Detective: How do you know Mr. Johnson is guilty? Bystander: I can't think of anyone else who would have committed the crime, so Mr. Johnson must have done it!
11. Studying symbolic logic is necessary in order to think clearly and coherently. Therefore, you ought to study symbolic logic.
12. Harvey: It is obvious people have free will. Bruno: How can you prove this? Harvey: What about the question you just asked me? Didn't you freely ask me a question?
13. Dogs and cats are mammals. Max is a cat and Rex is a dog. Therefore, Max and Rex are mammals.
14. Ever since the rise of the Internet in the nineties, the number of marriages in the United States has gone down. It is clear that the Internet is damaging traditional marriage.
15. Punk rock music is dangerous because it causes young people to question authority figures. If young people question authority figures, the political system will break down, and true democracy will cease to exist.
16. Socrates said, "The unexamined life is not worth living." Joan, who works at the mini mart, has obviously never examined her life. Therefore, her life is worthless.
17. People who convert to Catholicism only do so because they have an unconscious need for order and structure.
18. The new model of the computer is much faster than last year's model. It must be a far superior model.
19. Student to professor: You cannot give me a failing grade. I worked so hard in your class!

20. Student to professor: What are you going to do to help me succeed?

PART FIVE

Instructions: Answer the following questions about information presented in this book.

1. Which fallacy incorporates irrelevant information into the argument or discussion in order to distract?
2. Which fallacy presents the listener with only two options to choose from, when in fact there are more than two?
3. What type of argument assumes the whole is identical with its parts?
4. What type of communication is often easiest?
5. Which fallacy conflates truth with belief?
6. What type of argument contains an assumption that non-human things have human characteristics?
7. What type of fallacies involve the confusion of cause and effect?
8. Which argument simply restates its premise in a different way in its conclusion?
9. Which argument misrepresents another's position in order to dismiss it?
10. Which fallacy involves the assumption that a prescriptive statement can be derived from a purely descriptive statement?
11. Which fallacy incorporates name-calling or slander in order to manipulate the listener?
12. What attitude simply refuses to consider alternate possibilities and interpretations?
13. Which fallacy uses an appeal to pity?
14. Which fallacy is also known as the "democratic fallacy"? Why?
15. What type of argument incorporates threats or scare tactics?
16. Which fallacy involves a charge of hypocrisy?
17. Which fallacy occurs when a word having more than one meaning is used in two different ways in an argument?
18. Which argument appeals to something unknowable as evidence for its conclusion?
19. Which fallacy appeals to money or wealth?
20. Which fallacy occurs when one assumes two consecutive but independently occurring events, are causally related?

PART SIX

Instructions: Identify the valid and invalid argument forms in the following examples: Modus Ponens, Modus Tollens, Disjunctive Syllogism, Hypothetical Syllogism, Fallacy of Denying the Antecedent, and the Fallacy of Affirming the Consequent. If the argument does not take any of the forms, explain.

1. If I am late to work then I will lose my job. I am late to work. Therefore, I will lose my job.
2. Either we win the game, or we lose. If we win, then we stay in Atlanta. If we lose, then we go home to Chicago. So, either we stay in Atlanta or we go home to Chicago.
3. If the professor is late, then the class will be canceled. The class is not canceled. Therefore, the professor is not late.
4. If the unexamined life is not worth living, then I'd better start examining my life. If I start examining my life, then I'll need to question my beliefs. So, if the unexamined life is not worth living, then I'll need to question my beliefs.
5. Either empiricists are correct, or rationalists are correct. If empiricists are correct, then all knowledge is acquired through the senses. If rationalists are correct, then some knowledge is innate. So, either all knowledge is acquired through the senses or some knowledge is innate.
6. If Aristotle was Plato's student, then he was familiar with Plato's philosophy. Aristotle was Plato's student. So, Aristotle was familiar with Plato's philosophy.
7. Either Hegel was influenced by Marx or Marx was influenced by Hegel. Hegel was not influenced by Marx. Therefore, Marx must have been influenced by Hegel.
8. If we remain complacent, then we will be safe. If we fight for what is right, then we be persecuted. Either we will remain complacent or we will fight for what is right. So, we will either be safe, or we will be persecuted.
9. Understanding logic is necessary if one wants to recognize valid and invalid arguments. If understanding logic is necessary, then one will study it. Studying logic can be difficult, but if one wants to recognize valid arguments, then one will study logic.
10. If it is permissible for human beings to hunt animals for sport, then it is permissible for extraterrestrials to hunt human beings for sport. Humans have a long history of hunting animals for sport. It is permissible for humans to hunt animals for sport. Extraterrestrials do not hunt humans for sport, but it is permissible for them to do so.

11. Either Smith died from a gunshot wound or he died from a knife wound. It is not the case that Smith died from a knife wound. Therefore, Smith must have died from a gunshot wound.
12. If we continue to consume oil at our present rate, then we will run out by the year 2040. If we run out of oil by the year 2040, then we will need to design new technology or begin to use technology that does not rely on oil. So, if we continue to consume oil at our present rate, then we will need to design new technology or begin to use technology that does not rely on oil.
13. If Cartesians are rationalists, then they are skeptical of empiricism. Cartesians are skeptical of empiricism. Thus, Cartesians are rationalists.
14. If it rains, then Alex will take the train. It did not rain. Therefore, Alex will not take the train.
15. If John Searle's Chinese room argument is correct, then machines cannot think. If machines cannot think, then syntax doesn't suffice for semantics and artificial intelligence is not intelligent. So, If John Searle's Chinese room argument is correct, then then syntax doesn't suffice for semantics and artificial intelligence is not intelligent.

PART SEVEN

Instructions: Identify the fallacy or fallacies committed in the following quotations.

1. "Men should either be treated generously or destroyed, because they take revenge for slight injuries—for heavy ones they cannot."[1] Niccolo Machiavelli
2. "There are no facts, only interpretations."[2] Friedrich Nietzsche
3. "Democracy never lasts long. It soon wastes, exhausts, and murders itself. There never was a Democracy that did not commit suicide."[3] John Adams
4. "Religion is the sigh of the oppressed creature, the heart of a heartless world, just as it is the spirit of spiritless conditions. It is the opium of the people."[4] Karl Marx
5. "All religions, with their gods, demigods, prophets, messiahs and saints are the product of the fancy and the credulity of men who have not yet reached the full development and complete possession of their intellectual development."[5] Mikhail Bakunin
6. "If nature does not wish that weaker individuals should mate with the stronger, she wishes even less that a superior race should intermingle with an inferior one; because in such a case all her efforts, throughout

hundreds of thousands of years, to establish an evolutionary higher stage of being, may thus be rendered futile. History furnishes us with innumerable instances that prove this law."[6] Adolf Hitler

7. "Socialism is a philosophy of failure, the creed of ignorance, and the gospel of envy, its inherent virtue is the equal sharing of misery."[7] Winston Churchill
8. "What they have to discover, what all the efforts of capitalism's enemies are frantically aiming at hiding, is the fact that capitalism is not merely the 'practical,' but the only moral system in history."[8] Ayn Rand
9. "How do you tell a Communist? Well, it's someone who reads Marx and Lenin. And how do you tell an anti-Communist? It's someone who understands Marx and Lenin."[9] Ronald Reagan
10. "Indeed, I did have a relationship with Miss Lewinsky that was not appropriate. In fact, it was wrong. It constituted a critical lapse in judgment and a personal failure on my part for which I am solely and completely responsible. But I told the grand jury today and I say to you now that at no time did I ask anyone to lie, to hide or destroy evidence or to take any other unlawful action."[10] Bill Clinton
11. "Every nation in every region now has a decision to make. Either you are with us, or you are with the terrorists."[11] George W. Bush
12. "John McCain once opposed these tax cuts—he rightly called them unfair and fiscally irresponsible. But now he has done an about face and wants to make them permanent, just like he wants a permanent occupation in Iraq."[12] Barack Obama
13. "Crooked Hillary Clinton is the worst (and biggest) loser of all time. She just can't stop, which is good for the Republican Party. Hillary, get on with your life and give it another try in three years!"[13] Donald J. Trump
14. "Truly weird Senator Rand Paul of Kentucky reminds me of a spoiled brat without a properly functioning brain. He was terrible at [sic] DEBATE!"[14] Donald J. Trump
15. Journalist: "Should we allow the removal of the statue of Confederate Robert E. Lee in Charlottesville?" Trump: "What about George Washington? He was a slave owner. Are we going to take down statues of George Washington? How about Thomas Jefferson?"[15] Donald J. Trump

ANSWER KEY: PARTS TWO THROUGH SIX

Answers to all exercises are given below, except part one (create a fallacy) and part seven (fallacies in historical quotations).

PART TWO

1. Appeal to human nature
2. Fallacy of composition
3. Post hoc ergo propter hoc
4. Argumentum ad verecundiam
5. Anthropomorphism
6. Fallacy of composition
7. Appeal to anecdotal evidence
8. Complex question
9. Argumentum ad verecundiam
10. Argumentum ad baculum
11. Equivocation
12. Argumentum ad hominem, abusive
13. Ignoratio elenchi
14. Post hoc ergo propter hoc
15. Equivocation
16. Bifurcation
17. Bifurcation
18. Complex question
19. False certainty
20. Tu quoque

PART THREE

1. Is-ought fallacy
2. Perfectionist fallacy
3. Fallacy of definition; straw argument
4. Perfectionist fallacy
5. Argumentum ad hominem, circumstantial
6. Post hoc ergo propter hoc
7. Tu quoque
8. Two wrongs make a right
9. Shifting the burden of proof
10. Complex question
11. Appeal to consequences
12. Bifurcation; false dilemma
13. Appeal to anecdotal evidence
14. Subjectivist fallacy
15. Appeal to common knowledge
16. Argumentum ad verecundiam; fallacy of psychologism
17. Reductionism

18. Fallacy of definition
19. Complex question
20. Argumentum ad verecundiam

PART FOUR

1. Argumentum ad hominem, abusive
2. Argumentum ad ignorantiam
3. Not a fallacy
4. Petitio principii
5. Argumentum ad hominem, abusive
6. Equivocation
7. Not a fallacy
8. Argumentum ad populum
9. Petitio principii
10. Argumentum ad ignorantiam
11. Is-ought fallacy
12. Red herring
13. Not a fallacy
14. Post hoc ergo propter hoc
15. Slippery slope
16. Argumentum ad hominem, abusive
17. Fallacy of psychologism
18. Fallacy of efficiency
19. Ignoratio elenchi
20. Complex question

PART FIVE

1. Red herring
2. Bifurcation
3. Fallacy of composition
4. Vagueness
5. Subjectivist fallacy
6. Anthropomorphism
7. Causal fallacies
8. Petitio principii
9. Straw argument
10. Is-ought fallacy
11. Argumentum ad hominem, abusive
12. Willed ignorance
13. Argumentum ad misericordiam

14. Argumentum ad populum
15. Argumentum ad baculum
16. Tu quoque
17. Equivocation
18. Unknowable fact
19. Argumentum ad crumenam
20. Post hoc ergo propter hoc

PART SIX

1. Modus ponens
2. Constructive dilemma
3. Modus tollens
4. Hypothetical syllogism
5. Constructive dilemma
6. Modus ponens
7. Disjunctive syllogism
8. Constructive dilemma
9. Hypothetical syllogism
10. Modus ponens
11. Disjunctive syllogism
12. Hypothetical syllogism
13. Fallacy of affirming the consequent
14. Fallacy of denying the antecedent
15. Hypothetical syllogism

NOTES

1. Jay, Antony. (Editor) *Oxford Dictionary of Political Quotations*. Oxford: Oxford University Press, 2006. p. 250.
2. Ayer, A.J. & Jane O'Grady. (Editors) *A Dictionary of Philosophical Quotations*. Oxford: Blackwell, 1992. p. 318.
3. *Oxford Dictionary of Political Quotations*. p. 3.
4. *A Dictionary of Philosophical Quotations*. p. 285.
5. Bakunin, Mikhail. *God and State*. New York: Mother Earth Publishing Association. 1916. Chapter 2. From: www.marxists.org.
6. Hitler, Adolf. *Mein Kampf*. Translated by James Murphey. London: Hurst & Blackett, 1939. Chapter 11. From Project Gutenberg: www.gutenberg.org.
7. Churchill, Winston S. (Editor) *The Best of Winston Churchill's Speeches*. New York: Hyperion, 2003. p. 446.
8. Rand, Ayn. *Capitalism: The New Ideal*. New York: New American Library, 1966. p. 8
9. *Remarks at the Annual Convention of Concerned Women for America*, Sept. 25, 1987.
10. *Oxford Dictionary of Political Quotations*. p. 97.
11. *Address to a Joint Session of Congress and the American People*, Sept. 20, 2001.
12. Quoted by Answini Anburajan in "Obama: McCain Represents a Third Bush Term." From: www.msnbc.com. March 20, 2008.

13. Donald J. Trump, @RealDonaldTrump, Nov. 18, 2017.
14. Donald J. Trump, @RealDonaldTrump, Aug. 5, 2015.
15. Ryan Teague Beckworth, *Donald Trump's Favorite Dodge to a Tough Question: "What about . . . ?"* Time.com, Sept. 14, 2017.

Appendix II

Aristotle on the Law of Non-Contradiction

Aristotle (384–322 BCE) was the first philosopher in the classical world to write sustained works on logic. The importance of his work is monumental to the history of the Western intellectual tradition. He articulated in a clear and systematic manner the fundamental principles of logic, many of which are still used today in science, mathematics, and philosophy. For Aristotle, logic rests on, and stems from, the *law of non-contradiction*, which he discusses in the selections below. By understanding this axiomatic principle, one can clearly see the starting point of logic and valid argumentation.

While reading the following passages, one should ask: What is demonstration? What is a contradiction? What is a contradictory statement? Protagoras stated that all opinions and arguments are equal; how does Aristotle respond to this claim? What makes some opinions and/or arguments better than others?

The subsequent excerpts are from Aristotle's *Metaphysics*, Books IV and V. The translation used is by W. D. Ross (1908). Italics have been added.

EXCERPTS

There are some who, as we said, both themselves assert that it is possible for the same thing to be and not to be, and say that people can judge this to be the case. And among others many writers about nature use this language. But we have now posited that it is impossible for anything at the same time to be and not to be, and by this means have shown that *this is the most indisputable of all principles*. Some indeed demand that even this shall be demonstrated, but this they do through lack of education, for not to know of what things one should demand demonstration, and of what one should not, argues lack of education. For it is impossible that there should be demonstration of absolutely everything (there would be an infinite regress, so that there would still be no demonstration); but if there are things of which one should not demand demonstration, these persons could not say what principle they maintain to be more self-evident than the present one.

We can, however, demonstrate negatively even that this view is impossible, if our opponent will only say something; and if he says nothing, it is absurd to seek to give an account of our views to one who cannot give an account of anything, in so far as he cannot do so. For such a man, as such, is from the start no better than a vegetable. Now negative demonstration I distinguish from demonstration proper, because in a demonstration one might be thought to be begging the question, but if another person is responsible for the assumption, we shall have negative proof, not demonstration. The starting point for all such arguments is not the demand that our opponent shall say that something either is or is not (for this one might perhaps take to be a begging of the question), but that he shall say something which is significant both for himself and for another; for this is necessary, if he really is to say anything. For, if he means nothing, such a man will not be capable of reasoning, either with himself or with another. But if anyone grants this, demonstration will be possible; for we shall already have something definite. The person responsible for the proof, however, is not he who demonstrates but he who listens; for while disowning reason he listens to reason. And again, he who admits this has admitted that something is true apart from demonstration (so that not everything will be "so and not so").

First then this at least is obviously true, that the word "be" or "not be" has a definite meaning, so that not everything will be "so and not so." Again, if "man"' has one meaning, let this be "two-footed animal;" by having one meaning I understand this: if "man" means "X," then if A is a man "X" will be what "being a man" means for him. (It makes no difference even if one were to say a word has several meanings, if only they are limited in number; for to each definition there might be assigned a different word. For instance, we might say that "man" has not one meaning but several, one of which would have one definition, viz. "two-footed animal," while there might be also several other definitions if only they were limited in number; for a peculiar name might be assigned to each of the definitions. If, however, they were not limited but one were to say that the word has an infinite number of meanings, obviously reasoning would be impossible; *for not to have one meaning is to have no meaning, and if words have no meaning our reasoning with one another, and indeed with ourselves, has been annihilated*; for it is impossible to think of anything if we do not think of one thing; but if this is possible, one name might be assigned to this thing.)

Let it be assumed then, as was said at the beginning, that the name has a meaning and has one meaning; it is impossible, then, that "being a man" should mean precisely "not being a man," if "man" not only signifies something about one subject but also has one significance (for we do not identify "having one significance" with "signifying something about one subject," since on that assumption even "musical" and "white" and "man" would have had one significance, so that all things would have been one; for they would all have had the same significance).

And it will not be possible to be and not to be the same thing, except in virtue of an ambiguity, just as if one whom we call "man," others were to call "not-man"; but the point in question is not this, whether the same thing can at the same time be and not be a man in name, but whether it can in fact. Now if "man" and "not-man" mean nothing different, obviously "not being a man" will mean nothing different from "being a man"; so that "being a man" will be "not being a man"; for they will be one. For being one means this, being related as "raiment" and "dress" are, if their definition is one. And if "being a man" and "being a not-man" are to be one, they must mean one thing. But it was shown earlier' that they mean different things. Therefore, if it is true to say of anything that it is a man, it must be a two-footed animal (for this was what "man" meant); and if this is necessary, it is impossible that the same thing should not at that time be a two-footed animal; for this is what "being necessary" means, that it is impossible for the thing not to be. It is, then, impossible that it should be at the same time true to say the same thing is a man and is not a man.

The same account holds good with regard to "not being a man," for "being a man" and "being a not-man" mean different things, since even "being white" and "being a man" are different; for the former terms are much more different so that they must a fortiori mean different things. And if any one says that "white" means one and the same thing as "man," again we shall say the same as what was said before, that it would follow that all things are one, and not only opposites. But if this is impossible, then what we have maintained will follow, if our opponent will only answer our question.

And if, when one asks the question simply, he adds the contradictories, he is not answering the question. For there is nothing to prevent the same thing from being both a man and white and countless other things: but still, if one asks whether it is or is not true to say that this is a man, our opponent must give an answer which means one thing, and not add that "it is also white and large." For, besides other reasons, it is impossible to enumerate its accidental attributes, which are infinite in number; let him, then, enumerate either all or none. Similarly, therefore, even if the same thing is a thousand times a man and a not-man, he must not, in answering the question whether this is a man, add that it is also at the same time a not-man, unless he is bound to add also all the other accidents, all that the subject is or is not; and if he does this, he is not observing the rules of argument.

And in general, those who say this do away with substance and essence. For they must say that all attributes are accidents, and that there is no such thing as "being essentially a man" or "an animal." For if there is to be any such thing as "being essentially a man" this will not be "being a not-man" or "not being a man" (yet these are negations of it); for there was one thing which it meant, and this was the substance of something. And denoting the substance of a thing means that the essence of the thing is nothing else. But if its being essentially a man is to be the same as either being essentially a not-man or essentially not being a man, then its essence will be something else. Therefore, our opponents must say that there cannot be such a definition of anything, but that all attributes are accidental . . . But if all statements are accidental, there will be nothing primary about which they are made, if the accidental always implies predication about a subject. The predication, then, must go on ad infinitum. But this is impossible; for not even more than two terms can be combined in accidental predication.

. . . (A)gain, if all contradictory statements are true of the same subject at the same time, evidently all things will be one. For the same thing will be a trireme (a ship), a wall, and a man, if of everything it is possible either to affirm or to deny anything (and this premise must be accepted by those who share the views of Protagoras). For if anyone thinks that the man is not a trireme, evidently, he is not a trireme; so that he also is a trireme, if, as they say, contradictory statements are both true. And we thus get the doctrine of Anaxagoras, that all things are mixed together; so that nothing really exists. They seem, then, to be speaking of the indeterminate, and, while fancying themselves to be speaking of being, they are speaking about non-being; for it is that which exists potentially and not in complete reality that is indeterminate. But they must predicate of every subject the affirmation or the negation of every attribute. For it is absurd if of each subject its own negation is to be predicable, while the negation of something else which cannot be predicated of it is not to be predicable of it; for instance, if it is true to say of a man that he is not a man, evidently it is also true to say that he is either a trireme or not a trireme. If, then, the affirmative can be predicated, the negative must be predicable too; and if the affirmative is not predicable, the negative, at least, will be more predicable than the negative of the subject itself. If, then, even the latter negative is predicable, the negative of "trireme" will be also predicable; and, if this is predicable, the affirmative will be so too.

. . . (A)gain if when the assertion is true, the negation is false, and when this is true, the affirmation is false, it will not be possible to assert and deny the same thing truly at the same time. But perhaps they might say this was the very question at issue.

Again, is he in error who judges either that the thing is so or that it is not so, and is he right who judges both? If he is right, what can they mean by saying that the nature of existing things is of this kind? And if he is not right, but more right than he who judges in the other way, being will already be of a definite nature, and this will be true, and not at the same time also not true. *But if all are alike both wrong and right, one who is in this condition will not be able either to speak or to say anything intelligible; for he says at the same time both "yes" and "no."* And if he makes no judgement but "thinks" and "does not think," indifferently, what difference will there be between him and a vegetable? Thus, then, it is in the highest degree evident that neither any one of those who maintain this view nor anyone else is really in this position. For why does a man walk to Megara and not stay at home, when he thinks he ought to be walking there? Why does he not walk early some morning into a well or over a precipice, if one happens to be in his way? Why do we observe him guarding against this, evidently because he does not think that falling in is alike good and not good? Evidently, then, he judges one thing to be better and another worse. And if this is so, he must also judge one thing to be a man and another to be not-a-man, one thing to be sweet and another to be not-sweet. For he does not aim at and judge all things alike, when, thinking it desirable to drink water or to see a man, he proceeds to aim at these things; yet he ought, if the same thing were alike a man and not-a-man. *But, as was said, there is no one who does not obviously avoid some things and not others. Therefore, as it seems, all men make unqualified judgements, if not about all things, still about what is better and worse. And if this is not knowledge but opinion, they should be all the more anxious about the truth, as a sick man should be more anxious about his health than one who is healthy; for he who has opinions is, in comparison with the man who knows, not in a healthy state as far as the truth is concerned.*

Again, however much all things may be "so and not so," still there is a more and a less in the nature of things; for we should not say that two and three are equally even, nor is he who thinks four things are five equally wrong with him who thinks they are a thousand. If then they are not equally wrong, obviously one is less wrong and therefore more right. If, then, that which has more of any quality is nearer the norm, there must be some truth to which the more true is nearer. And even if there is not, still there is already something better founded and liker the truth, and we shall have got rid of the unqualified doctrine which would prevent us from determining anything in our thought.

From the same opinion proceeds the doctrine of Protagoras, and both doctrines must be alike true or alike untrue. For on the one hand, if all opinions and appearances are true, all statements must be at the same time true and false. For many men hold beliefs in which they conflict with one another, and think those mistaken who have not the same opinions as themselves; so that the same thing must both be and not be. And on the other hand, if this is so, all opinions must be true; for those who are mistaken and those who are right are opposed to one another in their opinions; if, then, reality is such as the view in question supposes, all will be right in their beliefs.

Evidently, then, both doctrines proceed from the same way of thinking. But the same method of discussion must not be used with all opponents; for some need persuasion, and others compulsion. Those who have been driven to this position by difficulties in their thinking can easily be cured of their ignorance; for it is not their expressed argument but their thought that one has to meet. But those who argue for the sake of argument can be cured only by refuting the argument as expressed in speech and in words.

Appendix III

Bertrand Russell on Truth and Falsehood

Bertrand Russell (1872–1970) was an influential twentieth-century philosopher. A prolific writer, Russell produced works on logic, mathematics, and the relationship between philosophy and contemporary society. In the following essay, Russell distinguishes between truth, falsehood, error, and belief. This text is of central importance for those studying logic—and fallacies in particular—because the concept of a logical fallacy presupposes a knowledge of truth, falsehood, error, and the like.

As students of philosophy, we should be able to clearly define the terms Russell discusses. As one reads the following essay, one should ask: What is knowledge by acquaintance? What is the definition of truth? What is falsehood? How is a belief related to truth? What is a fact? What is a judgment? By answering these questions, one will be well-equipped to engage further in the study of logic and philosophy.

The following essay, "On Truth and Falsehood," was first published in Russell's book, *The Problems of Philosophy* (1912).

EXCERPTS

Our knowledge of truths, unlike our knowledge of things, has an opposite, namely *error*. So far as things are concerned, we may know them or not know them, but there is no positive state of mind which can be described as erroneous knowledge of things, so long, at any rate, as we confine ourselves to knowledge by acquaintance. Whatever we are acquainted with must be something; we may draw wrong inferences from our acquaintance, but the acquaintance itself cannot be deceptive. Thus, there is no dualism as regards acquaintance. But as regards knowledge of truths, there is a dualism. We may believe what is false as well as what is true. We know that on very many subjects different people hold different and incompatible opinions: hence some beliefs must be erroneous. Since erroneous beliefs are often held just as strongly as true beliefs, it becomes a difficult question how they are to be distinguished from true beliefs. How are we to know, in a given case, that our belief is not erroneous? This is a question of the very greatest difficulty, to which no completely satisfactory answer is possible. There is, however, a preliminary question which is rather less difficult, and that is: What do we *mean* by truth and falsehood? It is this preliminary question which is to be considered in this chapter. In this chapter we are not asking how we can know whether a belief is true or false: we are asking what is meant by the question whether a belief is true or false. It is to be hoped that a clear answer to this question may help us to obtain an answer to the question what beliefs are true, but for the present we ask only "What is truth?" and "What is falsehood?" not "What beliefs are true?" and "What beliefs are false?" It is very important to keep these different questions entirely separate, since any confusion between them is sure to produce an answer which is not really applicable to either.

There are three points to observe in the attempt to discover the nature of truth, three requisites which any theory must fulfill.

1. Our theory of truth must be such as to admit of its opposite, falsehood. A good many philosophers have failed adequately to satisfy this condition: they have constructed theories according to which all our thinking ought to have been true, and have then had the greatest difficulty in finding a place for falsehood. In this respect our theory of belief must differ from our theory of acquaintance, since in the case of acquaintance it was not necessary to take account of any opposite.
2. It seems fairly evident that if there were no beliefs there could be no falsehood, and no truth either, in the sense in which truth is correlative to falsehood. If we imagine a world of mere matter, there would be no room for falsehood in such a world, and although it would contain what may be called "facts," it would not contain any truths, in the sense in which truths are things of the same kind as falsehoods. In fact, truth and falsehood are properties of beliefs and statements: hence a world of mere matter, since it would contain no beliefs or statements, would also contain no truth or falsehood.
3. But, as against what we have just said, it is to be observed that the truth or falsehood of a belief always depends upon something which lies outside the belief itself. If I believe that Charles I died on the scaffold, I believe truly, not because of any intrinsic quality of my

> belief, which could be discovered by merely examining the belief, but because of an historical event which happened two and a half centuries ago. If I believe that Charles I died in his bed, I believe falsely: no degree of vividness in my belief, or of care in arriving at it, prevents it from being false, again because of what happened long ago, and not because of any intrinsic property of my belief. Hence, although truth and falsehood are properties of beliefs, they are properties dependent upon the relations of the beliefs to other things, not upon any internal quality of the beliefs.

The third of the above requisites leads us to adopt the view—which has on the whole been commonest among philosophers—*that truth consists in some form of correspondence between belief and fact*. It is, however, by no means an easy matter to discover a form of correspondence to which there are no irrefutable objections. By this partly—and partly by the feeling that, if truth consists in a correspondence of thought with something outside thought, thought can never know when truth has been attained—many philosophers have been led to try to find some definition of truth which shall not consist in relation to something wholly outside belief. The most important attempt at a definition of this sort is the theory that truth consists in *coherence*. It is said that the mark of falsehood is failure to cohere in the body of our beliefs, and that it is the essence of a truth to form part of the completely rounded system which is The Truth.

There is, however, a great difficulty in this view, or rather two great difficulties. The first is that there is no reason to suppose that only *one* coherent body of beliefs is possible. It may be that, with sufficient imagination, a novelist might invent a past for the world that would perfectly fit on to what we know, and yet be quite different from the real past. In more scientific matters, it is certain that there are often two or more hypotheses which account for all the known facts on some subject, and although, in such cases, men of science endeavor to find facts which will rule out all the hypotheses except one, there is no reason why they should always succeed.

In philosophy, again, it seems not uncommon for two rival hypotheses to be both able to account for all the facts. Thus, for example, it is possible that life is one long dream, and that the outer world has only that degree of reality that the objects of dreams have; but although such a view does not seem inconsistent with known facts, there is no reason to prefer it to the common-sense view, according to which other people and things do really exist. Thus, coherence as the definition of truth fails because there is no proof that there can be only one coherent system.

The other objection to this definition of truth is that it assumes the meaning of "coherence" known, whereas, in fact, "coherence" presupposes the truth of the laws of logic. Two propositions are coherent when both may be true, and are incoherent when one at least must be false. Now in order to know whether two propositions can both be true, we must know such truths as the law of contradiction. For example, the two propositions, “this tree is a beech” and “this tree is not a beech,” are not coherent, because of the law of contradiction. But if the law of contradiction itself were subjected to the test of coherence, we should find that, if we choose to suppose it false, nothing will any longer be incoherent with anything else. Thus, the laws of logic supply the skeleton or framework within which the test of coherence applies, and they themselves cannot be established by this test.

For the above two reasons, coherence cannot be accepted as giving the *meaning* of truth, though it is often a most important *test* of truth after a certain amount of truth has become known.

Hence, we are driven back to *correspondence with fact* as constituting the nature of truth. It remains to define precisely what we mean by “fact,” and what is the nature of the correspondence which must subsist between belief and fact, in order that belief may be true.

In accordance with our three requisites, we have to seek a theory of truth which (1) allows truth to have an opposite, namely falsehood, (2) makes truth a property of beliefs, but (3) makes it a property wholly dependent upon the relation of the beliefs to outside things.

The necessity of allowing for falsehood makes it impossible to regard belief as a relation of the mind to a single object, which could be said to be what is believed. If belief were so regarded, we should find that, like acquaintance, it would not admit of the opposition of truth and falsehood, but would have to be always true. This may be made clear by examples. Othello believes falsely that Desdemona loves Cassio. We cannot say that this belief consists in a relation to a single object, “Desdemona’s love for Cassio,” for if there were such an object, the belief would be true. There is in fact no such object, and therefore Othello cannot have any relation to such an object. Hence his belief cannot possibly consist in a relation to this object.

It might be said that his belief is a relation to a different object, namely “that Desdemona loves Cassio”; but it is almost as difficult to suppose that there is such an object as this, when Desdemona does not love Cassio, as it was to suppose that there is “Desdemona’s love for Cassio.” Hence it will be better to seek for a theory of belief which does not make it consist in a relation of the mind to a single object.

It is common to think of relations as though they always held between two terms, but in fact this is not always the case. Some relations demand three terms, some four, and so on. Take, for instance, the relation “between.” So long as only two terms come in, the relation “between” is impossible: three terms are the smallest number that render it possible. York is between London and Edinburgh; but if London and Edinburgh were the only places in the world, there could be nothing which was between one place and another.

Similarly, *jealousy* requires three people: there can be no such relation that does not involve three at least. Such a proposition as "A wishes B to promote C's marriage with D" involves a relation of four terms; that is to say, A and B and C and D all come in, and the relation involved cannot be expressed otherwise than in a form involving all four. Instances might be multiplied indefinitely, but enough has been said to show that there are relations which require more than two terms before they can occur.

The relation involved in *judging* or *believing* must, if falsehood is to be duly allowed for, be taken to be a relation between several terms, not between two. When Othello believes that Desdemona loves Cassio, he must not have before his mind a single object, "Desdemona's love for Cassio" or "that Desdemona loves Cassio," for that would require that there should be objective falsehoods, which subsist independently of any minds; and this, though not logically refutable, is a theory to be avoided if possible. Thus it is easier to account for falsehood if we take judgment to be a relation in which the mind and the various objects concerned all occur severally; that is to say, Desdemona and loving and Cassio must all be terms in the relation which subsists when Othello believes that Desdemona loves Cassio. This relation, therefore, is a relation of four terms, since Othello also is one of the terms of the relation. When we say that it is a relation of four terms, we do not mean that Othello has a certain relation to Desdemona, and has the same relation to loving and also to Cassio. This may be true of some other relation than believing; but believing, plainly, is not a relation which Othello has to *each* of the three terms concerned, but to *all* of them together: there is only one example of the relation of believing involved, but this one example knits together four terms. Thus the actual occurrence, at the moment when Othello is entertaining his belief, is that the relation called "believing" is knitting together into one complex whole the four terms Othello, Desdemona, loving, and Cassio. What is called belief or judgment is nothing but this relation of believing or judging, which relates a mind to several things other than itself. An *act* of belief or of judgment is the occurrence between certain terms at some particular time, of the relation of believing or judging.

We are now in a position to understand what it is that distinguishes a true judgment from a false one. For this purpose we will adopt certain definitions. In every act of judgment there is a mind which judges, and there are terms concerning which it judges. We will call the mind the *subject* in the judgment, and the remaining terms the *objects*. Thus, when Othello judges that Desdemona loves Cassio, Othello is the subject, while the objects are Desdemona and loving and Cassio. The subject and the objects together are called the *constituents* of the judgment. It will be observed that the relation of judging has what is called a "sense" or "direction." We may say, metaphorically, that it puts its objects in a certain *order*, which we may indicate by means of the order of the words in the sentence. (In an inflected language, the same thing will be indicated by inflections, e.g. by the difference between nominative and accusative.) Othello's judgment that Cassio loves Desdemona differs from his judgment that Desdemona loves Cassio, in spite of the fact that it consists of the same constituents, because the relation of judging places the constituents in a different order in the two cases. Similarly, if Cassio judges that Desdemona loves Othello, the constituents of the judgment are still the same, but their order is different. This property of having a "sense" or "direction" is one which the relation of judging shares with all other relations. The "sense" of relations is the ultimate source of order and series and a host of mathematical concepts; but we need not concern ourselves further with this aspect.

We spoke of the relation called "judging" or "believing" as knitting together into one complex whole the subject and the objects. In this respect, judging is exactly like every other relation. Whenever a relation holds between two or more terms, it unites the terms into a complex whole. If Othello loves Desdemona, there is such a complex whole as "Othello's love for Desdemona." The terms united by the relation may be themselves complex, or may be simple, but the whole which results from their being united must be complex. Wherever there is a relation which relates certain terms, there is a complex object formed of the union of those terms; and conversely, wherever there is a complex object, there is a relation which relates its constituents. When an act of believing occurs, there is a complex, in which "believing" is the uniting relation, and subject and objects are arranged in a certain order by the "sense" of the relation of believing. Among the objects, as we saw in considering "Othello believes that Desdemona loves Cassio," one must be a relation—in this instance, the relation "loving." But this relation, as it occurs in the act of believing, is not the relation which creates the unity of the complex whole consisting of the subject and the objects. The relation "loving," as it occurs in the act of believing, is one of the objects—it is a brick in the structure, not the cement. The cement is the relation "believing." When the belief is *true*, there is another complex unity, in which the relation which was one of the objects of the belief relates the other objects. Thus, for example, if Othello believes *truly* that Desdemona loves Cassio, then there is a complex unity, "Desdemona's love for Cassio," which is composed exclusively of the *objects* of the belief, in the same order as they had in the belief, with the relation which was one of the objects occurring now as the cement that binds together the other objects of the belief. On the other hand, when a belief is *false*, there is no such complex unity composed only of the objects of the belief. If Othello believes *falsely* that Desdemona loves Cassio, then there is no such complex unity as "Desdemona's love for Cassio."

Thus, a belief is *true* when it *corresponds* to a certain associated complex, and *false* when it does not. Assuming, for the sake of definiteness, that the objects of the belief are two terms and a relation, the terms being put in a certain order by the "sense" of the believing, then if the two terms in that order are united by the relation into a complex, the belief is true; if not, it is false. This constitutes the definition of truth and falsehood that we were in search of. Judging or believing is a certain complex unity of which a mind is a constituent; if the remaining constituents, taken in the order which they have in the belief, form a complex unity, then the belief is true; if not, it is false.

Thus although truth and falsehood are properties of beliefs, yet they are in a sense extrinsic properties, for the condition of the truth of a belief is something not involving beliefs, or (in general) any mind at all, but only the *objects* of the belief. A mind, which believes, believes truly when there is a *corresponding* complex not involving the mind, but only its objects. This correspondence ensures truth, and its absence entails falsehood. Hence, we account simultaneously for the two facts that beliefs (a) depend on minds for their *existence*, (b) do not depend on minds for their *truth*.

We may restate our theory as follows: If we take such a belief as "Othello believes that Desdemona loves Cassio," we will call Desdemona and Cassio the *object-terms*, and loving the *object-relation*. If there is a complex unity "Desdemona's love for Cassio," consisting of the object-terms related by the object-relation in the same order as they have in the belief, then this complex unity is called the *fact corresponding to the belief*. Thus, a belief is true when there is a corresponding fact, and is false when there is no corresponding fact.

Minds do not *create* truth or falsehood. They create beliefs, but when once the beliefs are created, the mind cannot make them true or false, except in the special case where they concern future things which are within the power of the person believing, such as catching trains. What makes a belief true is a *fact*, and this fact does not (except in exceptional cases) in any way involve the mind of the person who has the belief.

Glossary of Logic and Critical Thinking Terms

Absolutism: The belief that there are certain unchanging and absolute truths. See *subjectivism*.

Analogy, argument from: An argument based on a likeness between two people, places, events, acts or things. Usually arguments from analogy are used in order to prove that, due to a similarity between two things, these things must be similar in other respects as well.

Anecdotal evidence: Support or evidence for a claim based on limited personal experience.

Antecedent: The "if" component of a conditional statement. The antecedent is always followed by the "then" part of the statement. See *conditional statement*.

Argument: In philosophy an argument is not a disagreement. Rather, an argument is a claim with reasons that are given in support. If a claim has no support, it is not an argument (see *assertion*). An argument is made up of two components: premises and a conclusion. See *premise* and *conclusion*.

Assertion: An unsupported claim.

Assumption: Usually an implicit or unstated belief. In logic, a built-in assumption is an unstated belief that is presupposed by the premises. For example: "I know that God exists because the bible states that he does." In this example, the premise ". . . because the bible states that he does" contains a built-in assumption: that the bible is correct.

Belief: A person or group's opinion or conviction about something. Beliefs can be true or false. One can believe that 2 + 2 = 7; this does not mean that it is true. Beliefs can also concern particular tastes or preferences, which are not objectively true or false.

Causal event: An event that is causally related to a following event, such as a pool cue hitting a billiard ball. See *non-causal event*.

Conclusion: The claim of an argument which uses premises as support.

Conditional statement: An "if-then" statement made up of an antecedent and a consequent. For example: "If it rains, then the car will get wet."

Conjunctive statement: A statement that combines two distinct components with an "and." For example: "Dave's family is German and Lutheran."

Consequent: The "then" component of a conditional statement, which always follows the "if" part of the statement. See *conditional statement*.

Contradiction: A contradiction occurs when two statements cannot both be true. For example, if one states that she has never been to London and that she has been to London, both of these statements cannot be true.

Deductive argument: An argument in which the conclusion is necessarily true if the premises are true and if the conclusion follows coherently from them.

Disanalogy: When an argument from analogy is weak due to a lack of similarity between things compared. Also known as a weak analogy.

Disjunctive statement: An "either-or" statement. For example: "Either Holmes solved the crime or Watson solved the crime."

Emotive language: Words or phrases specifically used in order to stimulate feelings.

Epistemology: The branch of philosophy that investigates questions concerning the nature, origin, and scope of knowledge.

Euphemism: A mild or inoffensive word or phrase substituted for a harsh or unpleasant fact or occurrence. For example, one might speak of "passing away" rather than dying.

Fact: Something that is indisputably true. For example, $2 + 3 = 5$ is a fact, and it is also a fact that the earth is spherical.

Fallacy: An error in reasoning or faulty reasoning. There are two types of fallacies: formal and informal.

Falsification: To establish the falsity of a conclusion by introducing a counter example that proves the conclusion false.

Formal fallacy: An argument that has a flaw in its structure, not in its content.

Hasty conclusion: A conclusion drawn from limited or insufficient evidence.

Inductive argument: An argument in which the truth of the conclusion is only probable.

Informal fallacy: An argument that contains a flaw in the content of the premises or conclusion. This often occurs due to built-in assumptions, omission or intrusion.

Informative language: Language that seeks to inform rather than to arouse feelings.

Invalid argument: A deductive argument in which the truth of the premises does not ensure the truth of the conclusion.

Law of non-contradiction: A basic law of logic stating that two statements cannot contradict each other and at the same time both be true. See *contradiction.*

Logic: The art or science of argumentation. Also, the study of methods used to arrive at correct conclusions.

Metaphysics: The branch of philosophy that investigates questions concerning the nature of reality, definitions of being, and causality.

Necessary condition: Any condition that, if absent, guarantees that an event will not occur. For example, a necessary condition for rain is the presence of clouds. (However, clouds do not guarantee that it will rain.) See *sufficient condition.*

Non-causal event: An event that does not necessarily have an effect, such as a coin toss. See *causal event.*

Non sequitur: Latin for "it does not follow." A non sequitur is any conclusion that does not follow logically from the premises.

Objective claim: A proposition that is not subjective. A truth claim that is not dependent on a specific individual's beliefs.

Philosophy: From the Greek, literally the "love of wisdom." To practice philosophy is to think critically and to question beliefs, knowledge, truth and other important aspects of human life. Socrates (470–399 BCE) is said to be the "father" of Western philosophy. His most famous statement was: "The unexamined life is not worth living" (Apology, 38a). A philosopher is one who sincerely examines his or her life and life itself.

Premise: Facts or evidence from which a conclusion is derived. Premises are the foundation upon which a conclusion rests.

Proposition: In logic, a proposition is not a proposal or plan. Rather, it is the truth or falsehood expressed in a sentence.

Rationalization: The practice of making an excuse for one's behavior even when one knows he or she is in the wrong.

Reductio ad absurdum: From the Latin "reduction to the absurd." An argument that claims a statement should be dismissed if its consequences are illogical or "absurd."

Reason: (1) Evidence or premises in an argument. (2) The human capacity to think logically and rationally.

Rhetoric: The art of persuasive speaking or writing. The rhetorician's primary concern is effectively persuading an audience. This may mean he or she is willing to use fallacious arguments, emotive language, and/or unsupported assertions in order to persuade.

Scapegoating: Occurs when one places the blame for a negative effect onto a person or group who are not responsible for it.

Semantics: The study of meaning in language. See *syntax*.

Signifier / Signified: A signifier is a word or linguistic term; the signified is the mental concept that the signifier represents. For example, one might use the word "God" (signifier) to represent the idea of a transcendent, all-powerful being (signified).

Soundness: An argument is sound when it is valid, and its premises are true.

Statement: A sentence that is either true or false.

Strong argument: An inductive argument in which is it probable, but not necessary, that the conclusion is true if indeed the premises are true.

Subjective claim: A proposition that is not objective. A truth claim that is dependent on a specific individual's beliefs.

Subjectivism: Also known as relativism. The belief that truth is entirely dependent on the subject or individual. See *absolutism*.

Sufficient condition: Any condition that, if present, guarantees that an event will occur. For example, decapitation of a human is a sufficient condition for death. In contrast, a gunshot is not a sufficient condition for death. One can be shot and still survive.

Syllogism: An argument made up of three components: two premises and a conclusion. The most famous example is:

Premise 1: All humans are mortal.
Premise 2: Socrates is a human.
Conclusion: Socrates is mortal.

Syntax: The rules and characteristics of sentence structure. See *semantics*.

Truth: In logic, a belief, statement, or proposition is true if it accurately describes how things actually are.

Valid argument: An argument with valid structure or form. A deductive argument is valid if the truth of the premises logically ensures the truth of the conclusion. Validity is not a guarantor of truth, however. An argument may be valid and also contain false premises.

Verification: To establish the truth of a conclusion by empirical observation.

Weak argument: An inductive argument in which it is unlikely that the conclusion is true, even if the premises are true.

Recommended Reading

One of the most helpful introductions to formal, informal, and categorical logic is C. Stephen Layman's *The Power of Logic*. A more recent edition is available with revisions by Frances Howard-Snyder, Daniel Howard-Snyder, and Ryan Wasserman. This textbook provides short, clear chapters on the basics of logic and critical thinking.

If one is looking for an inexpensive guide to critical thinking and logical terms, one should turn to Nigel Warburton's *Thinking from A to Z*. This is a small book that can be thrown in a backpack and used for reference in the college classroom or anywhere else.

One of my favorite books on informal logical fallacies is Madsen Pirie's *The Book of the Fallacy: A Handbook for Intellectual Subversives*. This is out of print, but a new edition has been released under a new title: *How to Win Every Argument: The Use and Abuse of Logic*. While I prefer the older edition, this book provides a good overview of many informal logical fallacies.

A very helpful historical overview of the development of logic is found in William and Martha Kneale's *The Development of Logic*. This is a clear survey of the evolution of Western logic from Aristotle, through Scholasticism, and into the present era. Another useful history text is Anton Dumitriu's *History of Logic*. Dumitriu gives an insightful introduction not only to Western logic but also to Indian and Chinese logic.

If one is looking to learn more about Indian logic, philosopher Bilal Krishna Matilal has written and edited several helpful books, including *The Character of Logic in India*. Also, of interest is the *Nyāya-sūtra: Selections with Early Commentaries*, edited by Matthew Dasti and Steven Phillips; it gives a solid overview of classical Indian rhetoric, logic, and rules of rational debate. For Chinese logic, a highly recommended title is Brian Carr and

Indira Mahalingam's edited volume, *Companion Encyclopedia of Asian Philosophy*. There are several helpful essays in the volume, including "Logic and Language in Chinese Philosophy," by Zhang Chunpo and Zhang Jialong.

Finally, for general information about logical terms, debates, and the history of logic, a helpful online resource is the Stanford Encyclopedia of Philosophy: plato.stanford.edu.

Bibliography

Ackrill, J. L. *Aristotle's Categories and De Interpretatione, Clarendon Aristotle Series*. Oxford: Clarendon Press, 1961.

Aristotle. *On Sophistical Refutations. On Coming-to-Be and Passing Away. On the Cosmos.* Translated by E. S. Forster and D. J. Furley. Cambridge: Harvard University Press, 1955.

———. *Posterior Analytics*. Translated by Hugh Treddenick and E. S. Forster. Cambridge: Harvard University Press, 1960.

———. *Prior Analytics*. Translated by Robin Smith. Indianapolis: Hackett, 1989.

Ayer, Alfred J. *Language, Truth and Logic*. New York: Dover, 1952.

Ayer, Alfred J. and Jane O'Grady. (Editors) *A Dictionary of Philosophical Quotations*. Oxford: Blackwell, 1992.

Baron, Jonathan. *Thinking and Deciding.* Third Edition. New York: Cambridge University Press, 2000.

Beaney, Michael. (Editor) *The Oxford Handbook of the History of Analytic Philosophy*. Oxford: Oxford University Press, 2013.

Bochenski, I.M. *History of Formal Logic*. Translated by Ivo Thomas. Notre Dame: University of Notre Dame Press, 1961.

Cassell's Latin Dictionary, compiled by D. P. Simpson. New York: Macmillan, 1977.

Carnap, Rudolph. *Logical Foundations of Probability*. Chicago: University of Chicago Press, 1950.

Carr, Brian and Indira Mahalingham. (Editors) *Companion Encyclopedia of Asian Philosophy*. London: Routledge, 1997.

Copi, Irving M. *Introduction to Logic*. Sixth Edition. New York: Macmillan, 1986.

Dasti, Matthew and Stephen Phillips. (Editors) *The Nyāya-sūtra: Selections with Early Commentaries*. Cambridge: Hackett, 2017.

Detlefsen, Michael and David Charles McCarty and John B. Bacon. *Logic from A to Z*. London: Routledge, 1999.

Dumitriu, Anton. *History of Logic*. London: Routledge, 1977.

Edwards, Paul. "Heidegger's Quest for Being," in *Philosophy*, 1989. 64: 437–470.

Ellul, Jacques. *Propaganda: The Formation of Men's Attitudes*. Translated by Konrad Kellen. New York: Vintage, 1965.

Feibleman, James K. *Assumptions of Grand Logics*. The Hague: Martinus Nijhoff, 1979.

Fisher, Jennifer. *On the Philosophy of Logic*. Belmont, CA: Wadsworth, 2008.

Ganeri, Jonardon. (Editor) *Indian Logic: A Reader*. New York: Routledge, 2001.

Gokhale, Pradeep P. *Inference and Fallacies Discussed in Ancient Indian Logic (With Special Reference to Nyāya and Buddhism)*. Delhi: Sri Satguru Publications, 1992.

Haack, Susan. *A Philosophy of Logics*. Cambridge: Cambridge University Press, 1978.

Hamblin, C. L. *Fallacies*. London: Methuen & Co., 1970.
Heidegger, Martin. *Being and Time*. Translated by John Macquarrie and Edward Robinson. New York: Harper, 1962.
———. *An Introduction to Metaphysics*. Translated by Ralph Mannheim. New Haven: Yale University Press, 1972.
———. *The Metaphysical Foundations of Logic*. Translated by Michael Heim. Bloomington: Indiana University Press, 1984.
Herrick, Paul. *The Many Worlds of Logic*. Second Edition. Oxford: Oxford University Press, 2000.
Hume, David. *An Enquiry Concerning Human Understanding*. Cambridge: Hackett, 1977.
Husserl, Edmund. *Formal and Transcendental Logic*. Translated by Dorion Cairns. The Hague: Martinus Nijhoff, 1977.
———. *The Shorter Logical Investigations*. Translated by J. N. Findlay. New York: Routledge, 2001.
Jay, Antony. (Editor) *The Oxford Dictionary of Political Quotations*. Oxford: Oxford University Press, 2006.
Kant, Immanuel. *Critique of Pure Reason*. Translated by Norman Kemp Smith. New York: St. Martin's, 1965.
———. *Lectures on Logic*. Edited by J. Michael Young. Cambridge: Cambridge University Press, 1992.
Kneale, William and Martha Kneale. *The Development of Logic*. Oxford: Clarendon Press, 1985.
Laplanch, J. and J.-B. Pontalis. *The Language of Psycho-Analysis*. Translated by Donald Nicholson-Smith. London: The Hogarth Press, 1980.
Layman, C. Stephen. *The Power of Logic*. Third Edition. New York: McGraw- Hill, 2005.
Lewis, C. S. *The Case for Christianity*. New York: Scribner, 1989.
Matilal, B. K. *The Character of Logic in India*. Albany: State University of New York Press, 1998.
Malpass, Alex and Marianna Antonutti Marfori. (Editors) *The History of Philosophical and Formal Logic: From Aristotle to Tarski*. New York: Bloomsbury Academic, 2017.
McInerny, D. Q. *Being Logical: A Guide to Good Thinking*. New York: Random House, 2005.
Merleau-Ponty, Maurice. *Phenomenology of Perception*. Translated by Donald A. Landes. New York: Routledge, 2012.
Mohanty, J. N. *Classical Indian Philosophy*. Lanham, MD: Rowman & Littlefield, 2000.
Moore, Brooke Noel and Richard Parker. *Critical Thinking*. Twelfth Edition. New York: McGraw-Hill, 2016.
Parry, William T. and Edward A. Hacker. *Aristotelian Logic*. New York: State University of New York Press, 1991.
Pirie, Madsen. *The Book of the Fallacy: A Handbook for Intellectual Subversives*. London: Routledge, 1970.
———. *How to Win Every Argument: The Use and Abuse of Logic*. London: Continuum, 2006.
Plato. *Protagoras*. Translated by Stanley Lombardo and Karen Bell. Cambridge: Hackett, 1992.
———. *Republic*. Translated by C. D. C. Reeve. Cambridge: Hackett, 2004.
———. *Sophist*. Translated by Nicholas P. White. Cambridge: Hackett, 1993.
Potter, Michael. *Wittgenstein's Notes on Logic*. Oxford: Oxford University Press, 2011.
Rolf, Bertil. "A Theory of Vagueness," in *Journal of Philosophical Logic*, 1980. 9: 315–325.
Russell, Bertrand. *Mysticism and Logic*. New York: Anchor, 1963.
———. *Problems of Philosophy*. Cambridge: Hackett, 1972.
———. *Why I am Not a Christian and Other Essays on Religion and Related Subjects*. New York: Simon & Schuster, 1967.
Schum, David. *The Evidential Foundations of Probabilistic Reasoning*. New York: Wiley & Sons, 1994.
Searle, John. "How to Derive 'Ought' from 'Is,'" in *Philosophical Review*, 1964. 73: 43–58.
———. *Speech Acts: An Essay on the Philosophy of Language*. Cambridge: Cambridge University Press, 1969.

Smart, Ninian. *Doctrine and Argument in Indian Philosophy*. London: George Allen & Unwin, 1964.

Soccio, Douglas J. & Vincent E. Barry. *Practical Logic: An Antidote for Uncritical Thinking*. Fifth Edition. Belmont: Wadsworth, 1998.

Sorenson, Roy A. *Blindspots*. Oxford: Clarendon Press, 1988.

Thom, Paul. *The Syllogism*. Munich: Philosophia Verlag, 1983.

Van Vleet, Jacob E. *Informal Logical Fallacies: A Brief Guide*. Lanham, MD: University Press of America, 2010.

Walton Douglas and Alan Brinton. *Historical Foundations of Informal Logic*. London: Ashgate, 1997.

Walton, Douglas H. *Abductive Reasoning*. Tuscaloosa: University of Alabama Press, 2013.

———. *Burden of Proof, Presumption, and Argumentation*. Cambridge: Cambridge University Press, 2014.

———. *Fundamentals of Argumentation*. Cambridge: Cambridge University Press, 2005.

———. *Informal Logic: A Handbook for Critical Argumentation*. Cambridge: Cambridge University Press, 1989.

———. *Methods of Argumentation*. Cambridge: Cambridge University Press, 2013.

Warburton, Nigel. *Thinking from A to Z*. Third Edition. London: Routledge, 2007.

Weston, Anthony. *A Rulebook for Arguments*. Fifth Edition. Cambridge: Hackett, 2018.

Whitaker, C. W. A. *Aristotle's De Interpretatione: Contradiction and Dialectic*. Oxford: Clarendon Press, 1996.

Wittgenstein, Ludwig. *Culture and Value*. Translated by Peter Winch. Chicago: University of Chicago Press, 1980.

———. *Lectures and Conversations on Aesthetics, Psychology, and Religious Belief*. Edited by Cyril Barrett. Berkeley: University of California Press, 1967.

———. *On Certainty*. Translated by G.E.M. Anscombe and G.M. von Wright. New York: Harper & Row, 1972.

———. *Philosophical Investigations*. Translated by G. E. M. Anscombe. Oxford: Blackwell, 1973.

———. *Tractatus Logico-Philosophicus*. Translated by D. F. Pears and B. F. McGuinness. London: Routledge, 1974.

Wuellner, Bernard. *Dictionary of Scholastic Philosophy*. Fitzwilliam, NH: Loreto, 2013.

Index

About the Author

Jacob E. Van Vleet is professor of philosophy at Diablo Valley College located in the San Francisco Bay Area. He is the author of *Dialectical Theology and Jacques Ellul* and co-author of *Jacques Ellul: A Companion to His Major Works*.